❀ ı ❀ ı ❀ ı ❀ ı ❀ ı ❀ ı ❀ ı ❀ ı ❀ ı ❀ ı ❀ ı ❀ ı ❀

RASPBERRY PI

A Comprehensive Beginner's Guide to Setup, Programming (Concepts and Techniques) and Developing Cool Raspberry Pi Projects

❀ ı ❀ ı ❀ ı ❀ ı ❀ ı ❀ ı ❀ ı ❀ ı ❀ ı ❀ ı ❀ ı ❀ ı ❀

Joe Grant

Table of Contents

❋ I ❋ I ❋ I ❋ I ❋ I ❋ I ❋ I ❋ I ❋ I ❋ I ❋ I ❋ I ❋ I ❋

Introduction

❋ ｜ ❋ ｜ ❋ ｜ ❋ ｜ ❋ ｜ ❋ ｜ ❋ ｜ ❋ ｜ ❋ ｜ ❋ ｜ ❋ ｜ ❋ ｜ ❋ ｜ ❋ ｜ ❋

Congratulations on purchasing your very own copy of *Raspberry Pi: A Comprehensive Beginner's Guide to Setup, Programming (Concepts and Techniques) and Developing Cool Raspberry Pi Projects*. The purpose of this book is to reveal a fun, easy way to learn programming while creating entertaining projects.

Learning how to program and working with tech can be tedious at times, and that is why many students give up in the middle of the process. This book explores this issue and offers a credit card-sized computer as the answer. The Raspberry Pi is a small, easy to use computer that can be utilized to create anything from a simple security camera to a professional home security system. Having a cool project as your focus will push you to learn how to program, because programming on its own feels sterile. Having something to look forward to will drive your thirst for knowledge.

The main objective of *Raspberry Pi: A Comprehensive Beginner's Guide* is to teach you everything about Raspberry Pi, the basics of working with the Linux operating system, and to guide you through learning how to program with Python. Do not allow yourself to be

1

overwhelmed by so much information, as you will take it in step by step. The book is meant for a beginner. There will be some exercises and examples included to help you solidify your basic knowledge of programming and at the end of the book, we'll take a look at some of the cool projects we can make with the Pi.

Get the most out of the information you are about to absorb by putting it into practice as soon as possible. Knowledge requires implementation in order to be truly useful, and that is even more valid when it comes to programming. It might not be easy at first, but each chapter will carefully guide you and teach you everything you need to know in order to get started with your very own Raspberry Pi.

Chapter 1

Setup

❋ ❙ ❋ ❙ ❋ ❙ ❋ ❙ ❋ ❙ ❋ ❙ ❋ ❙ ❋ ❙ ❋ ❙ ❋ ❙ ❋ ❙ ❋ ❙ ❋ ❙ ❋ ❙ ❋

You've got your hands on a Raspberry Pi computer - but do you know where to start? Do you know anything about the device? Are you familiar with its operating system? Do you have programming skills in any language, or specifically in Python? Are you perhaps an occasional tech user who became curious about computers and programming? No matter the case, this chapter's purpose is to get you started on the right path. Even if you are familiar with the Raspberry Pi and already know how to set it up, you might want to refresh your knowledge.

The Raspberry Pi has existed for several years already, but many people aren't aware of it because they grew so accustomed to relying on Windows or MAC based personal computers. Even some programmers and software developers are shocked to find out that they could've started out on a computer that is cheaper than a night out. However, this doesn't mean that it's not popular. With every year, more and younger would-be programmers start out practicing on such a device. It is affordable and easy to work with. So if you're still thinking about purchasing a Raspberry Pi, start browsing for one. It is the ideal computer for learning programming, and there are so many cool projects you can create with it. Plus, you already got your hands on this book, so how else will you complete the projects in the last chapter if you don't have your own Pi?

Let's start exploring the Raspberry Pi and learn how to perform a proper setup. In this chapter, you will learn more about this type of computer and its components, and you will learn how to put it together. Don't be alarmed - you don't need expert tech skills to set it up.

Explore the Raspberry Pi

You must be very excited to get started, but you shouldn't rush into things. It's important to first understand the device and its components. First you need to know that there are three main board types and several computer models. If you already bought yours, you should check out the model and then continue reading.

The Pi comes in three flavors: Model A, Model B, and Model Zero. They share a few components and each of them can suit a different purpose, depending on your project. Let's take a look at some of the specs to be able to tell them apart and decide on which project to use them for.

Raspberry Pi Model A+

As we mentioned, the first computer model is model A, or model A+ to be more specific. Model A has been discontinued and A+ took on its role. This revision of the original is smaller, uses 32 bit architecture, and comes with a single core processor, a Broadcom BCM2835 System on a Chip and 512 MB of RAM. The graphics from this model are present on every other model as well. Other notable features are the single USB port, a camera serial interface connector, an HDMI port, video-audio input ports for LCD screens, and a micro SD card slot. The A+ also comes with a 40 pin array which can be used to connect a variety of electronics, depending on your project.

If you already have this model, you might consider using it for a security camera design with a motion sensor. It can also work on a weather balloon project or as a robot brain.

Raspberry Pi Model B+

The B+ board is bigger than model A and can suit a larger number of purposes due to the added connectivity options. It uses a 32 bit architecture just like model A, but it comes with 4 USB slots and an Ethernet port. Every other feature is the same as on the A+ version, however, it comes with a micro SDHC slot instead of a regular micro SD, so you'll have the option of using high speed cards.

This model is recommended for a basic server setup. For example, you can use it to run a wireless print server or as a tool for network monitoring.

Raspberry Pi 2 Model B

This version is identical to model B+ when it comes with design, but you get a much faster processor and more RAM. It comes with a quad core, 900 MHz CPU instead of a single core, a Broadcom

BCM2837 System on a Chip and 1GB of RAM. This is a massive upgrade and can be used for many projects. For instance, if you're feeling nostalgic or retro, you can run and play the original Doom without using an emulator.

Raspberry Pi 3 Model B

This model is a further improvement of the B model board. It has the same dimensions, but the quad core processor comes with a 1.2 GHz chip. This Raspberry Pi version is also the first one to feature a wireless connection and onboard Bluetooth without requiring any external devices to be connected.

You can use this model for any project as long as you have the room for it. It is powerful, and many hobbyists love using it for recreating retro game stations.

Raspberry Pi Zero Models

These models live up to the name from every point of view. Firstly, they cost almost zero by having a price tag of around $5. Secondly, they weigh almost zero - these computers come in at only 9 grams. Both of these advantages are great for any project where space is very limited. However, this doesn't mean that the computer isn't powerful enough.

The basic Pi zero comes with a 1GHz single core processor, a 32 bit architecture and 512 MB of RAM. All Zero models use the same System on a Chip as model A+ and B+. You also find a micro USB for data and one for power, as well as a micro HDMI connection and a micro SD card slot.

There are two other variations of this model with a few extra features that may come in handy.

The Raspberry Pi Zero W is basically the same as the base model, but it also features wireless connectivity and Bluetooth. If you need to establish a remote connection for your project, then this model is suited for the task.

The Raspberry Pi Zero WH is nearly the same as the W version. The only difference is that the WH comes with GPIO pins.

All of these Zero models have been designed to be used in projects where you don't have much space, or the weight you can introduce is very limited. So take your pick!

Understanding the Components

As previously mentioned at the beginning of this chapter, this part of the book is intended to be helpful even to the least tech savvy person out there. To accomplish this, we will discuss all the components in a little more detail. Building a solid foundation is important in order to fully understand how the Raspberry Pi works and what you can do with it.

The SD Card

Raspberry Pi's don't come with onboard hard drives like you are used to seeing in other computers and in laptops. There is no room to attach such a device. The main feature of the Pi at the end of the day is its size. This is why an SD Card is used instead. You can store a vast amount of information in such a tiny space that weighs nearly nothing.

How much space do you really need? Well, that depends on your project, however it's recommended to use at least 2 to 4 GB SD Cards. They are inexpensive and you need to make sure you have plenty of room for the software you are going to use. If you want more, you can easily go up to 32 GBs and even beyond, though you probably don't have the need for so much memory space.

The Micro Power Port

All computers need power, and the Pi is no exception. However, you don't need a heavy power supply attached to it like with many PCs. A smartphone charger is all you really need to get it powered and ready to use.

If you're inventive, you can even use regular batteries to power the Pi, though it's not really recommended because the power will either fluctuate or run out fairly quickly. There are, however, situations when this powering method can come in handy. We'll discuss this in a later chapter.

The System on a Chip

Or SoC for short. This component is what integrates all the other components in the Raspberry Pi. You can find this system in today's mobile devices as well because of how small and energy efficient it is. If you are familiar with laptops and computers, you know about the motherboard, which houses all the components and parts. In the case of the motherboard, all devices are detachable.

The SoC, however, integrates all of the parts into a single integrated circuit.

The HDMI, Ethernet and USB Ports

The Raspberry Pi comes with an HDMI port which allows you to connect to a high definition display. Together with the onboard graphics processing unit, the Pi can handle Blu-ray quality 1080p graphics.

With Ethernet and USB support, the Pi can function pretty much the same way as any other computer you are used to. You can connect a webcam, a router, or even an external hard drive or solid state drive. This makes the machine highly versatile and usable in many projects.

GPIO Pins

We mentioned these pins earlier, but what are they for exactly? They are General Purpose Input Output pins, hence GPIO, and they allow you to connect a wide variety of electronic devices. This part of the Pi is absolutely vital, because it allows you to implement the computer into so many projects. You can connect LED lights, servo motors, extension boards and pretty much anything else you can imagine.

A day to day computer like your desktop PC doesn't allow you such easy access to connecting any device you want. You would have to really dig in to make anything work, and it can take a lot of time and experimentation. With the Raspberry Pi, you already have access to the pins with a bit of Python or C programming knowledge. For instance, as soon as you get your hands on a Pi, you can connect several motors and create a robot pet. You can't really do that with a laptop or desktop.

Putting Everything Together

The first thing you need is power. The Raspberry Pi needs 5V of steady energy. You can improvise with a phone charger because most of them have an output of 5V, or you can simply buy a power supply designed to be used with the Pi. You can ask at any electronic store, or buy the power supply from the same place you ordered your Pi. Follow the guidelines on your model, because if you don't get an adequate power supply you might encounter random issues. For instance, when you connect a keyboard, your mouse might lose power and stop working. You don't want to have to deal with that in the middle of a project.

Next up, you should connect a monitor, because from here onwards you need to see what you're doing. You can use the HDMI port to connect any monitor, and if yours comes only with DVI capabilities, just use a converter. In the tech world, compatibility shouldn't be a big issue because there's a converter for everything.

Depending on your chosen model, you might have a limited number of USB ports. You need them for a mouse, a keyboard, a wireless connection, and more. So even if your Pi came with just one USB port, don't worry, just connect a USB hub with as many ports as you want. Power can become a problem here because the hub demands it, as well as all the other devices you attach to the hub. You might want to consider getting a USB port hub that you can power outside of using the Pi. This way you won't risk any power fluctuations.

That's it for now, but as a final step, you might want to consider enclosing your Pi. You know how your PC comes in a big case? Well, most Raspberry Pi's come bare bones with no case and no protection whatsoever. This can leave the device vulnerable because of all the exposed connections. You can even cause a short because the circuit board is not protected and if it comes in contact with metal, it fries.

The type of case you get is a matter of taste, but before you settle you should consider the need for quick access to the GPIO pins and ventilation. If you plan to connect various electronics to the Pi, you need a type of case that lets you attach devices without disassembling everything. Ventilation is also crucial because every computer generates heat, especially if you plan to use it for video game projects.

The Operating System

The Raspberry Pi is designed to work with Linux as its operating system. If you have no experience with Linux, that's perfectly alright. We will talk about in detail in the second chapter. In this section, we'll just go through the basics to get the computer running.

First, you need to know that there are a variety of Linux versions, or distributions as they're actually called. The one you are looking for is aptly named Raspbian.

But the Raspberry Pi doesn't come with a hard drive, so how do you install the operating system? You need to use an SD card. Download and copy a disk image of Raspbian to your card and the Pi will use it to boot up the system. It's advisable to use a high quality, high speed SD card with plenty of memory, at least 4GBs. Not all SD cards are the same, so choose a respectable brand and aim for speed in order to boot your system as fast as possible.

The next step is to format your SD card. Your Pi can't read it yet without performing this step, so you need to use a Windows or a Mac computer for formatting. All you need to do is download an SD formatting tool and follow the given steps. If you don't want to go through the hassle of formatting and writing SD cards, you always have the option to buy an already formatted card with the operating system preinstalled.

Configuration

Once you're done setting up the SD card and have installed Raspbian, you can boot up your Raspberry Pi for the first time. When you start up the computer, you will be welcomed by a configuration tool called raspi-config. Here you will have various configuration options over which you have full control. The basic options include an expansion of the file system, creation of a user password, and processor overclocking. Choose to modify anything you like, however, be careful with the overclocking. We'll discuss this option in further detail later, but for now you should keep in mind that you can shorten the lifespan of the Pi by overclocking too much.

The configuration tool also comes with advanced options such as creating a host name and memory splitting. Here you should enable SSH access because you will need it later. At this stage, you should explore all the options and play with them to get more accustomed to the Pi. Nothing bad can happen to your Pi at this point. In the worst case scenario, your SD card could stop working properly, but it's not as bad as it sounds. If you do something that makes it unusable, you will simply have to reformat the card, nothing else.

When you're done fiddling with the configuration tool, hit the "Finish" button to finish the actual installation and configuration of the operating system. If you are greeted by a command line interface, don't worry, that's not how you need to use the computer. It just means you forgot to enable the desktop environment in the configuration tool. You should type in your username and password in the command line if you already customized them. If you didn't set them up, do the following:

1. Type *$ pl* as your username.

2. Type *$ raspberry* as your password.

3. Type *$ startx* to enter the desktop environment.

Now you should see a familiar user interface similar to when you start up your Windows or Mac computer. You will see programs and file icons such as Midori, a web browser, or IDLE, for working in Python.

Bravo! You successfully assembled and booted your very own Raspberry Pi. Next up, you should check whether everything is up to date. Raspbian updates the same way Windows does. In order to update the OS, use the command line prompt and type *$ sudo apt-get update*. The computer will refresh its software list at this point and when it's done, you need to type *$ sudo apt-get upgrade*. If there's any update available to you, the Pi will ask you to confirm that you wish to update the software. Hit the "Enter" button to confirm the update and restart the computer.

How to Shut Down

Now that you know how to start up your Pi and how to perform some basic navigation, you need to learn how to shut it down. You don't have an on and off switch, after all. Firstly, the Raspberry Pi consumes such a tiny amount of power that shutting it off isn't really necessary, but doing so might increase its lifespan.

Once you're done using the computer, simply unplug it. Won't this harm the Pi? No, it's designed this way. There's no danger of causing any damage, but if you still worry about pulling out the cord, there's another way that might ease the tension.

Open the console and type *$ sudo shutdown -r now*. The computer will run through all the shutdown procedures, closing processes one by one, just like a Mac or Windows PC. Depending on the Raspberry Pi model, the device might take you back to a black screen with a text only user interface. If you reach this page, you can unplug the computer.

Performance and Overclocking

What is overclocking? This process refers to boosting an electronic device, usually a computer processor, to run faster than it's intended by the manufacturer. It involves increasing the clock frequency, which is measured in megahertz. Overclocking is usually performed when a processor isn't running as fast as it can. The manufacturer locks it at a limit which is considered safe, however it can be pushed further. Take note that overclocking is the best way to boost a processor's performance, however, it usually lowers its lifespan. Don't overclock your device unless you really need the extra juice for a project.

The Raspberry Pi can be overclocked like any other computer, and doing so can increase its processing power considerably. Keep in mind that the device will also generate more heat, so make sure the casing is ventilated before overclocking.

So how do you do it? The only safe way is to dynamically overclock the Pi. This means that when the processor starts running too hot, beyond the safety limit, the clock speed will be automatically reduced to lower the heat generation. To start overclocking, you need to run your Pi's configuration tool, raspi_config, by typing *$ sudo raspi-config* in the command console. When you open the tool, choose the option to overclock and then choose one of the presets offered by the computer. Play with these options to find the most suitable choice. If your Pi starts lagging or stalling, then you need to kick it down a notch and go with a lower preset.

Chapter 2

Understanding Linux Basics

❋ ❙ ❋ ❙ ❋ ❙ ❋ ❙ ❋ ❙ ❋ ❙ ❋ ❙ ❋ ❙ ❋ ❙ ❋ ❙ ❋ ❙ ❋ ❙ ❋ ❙ ❋ ❙ ❋

Linux

A s previously mentioned, the Raspberry Pi runs by using Linux as its operating system. If you've only used Windows or Mac until now, don't worry. This chapter will be dedicated to helping you understand how to operate this system.

Linux has been vastly improved over the years, because it didn't use to be the most user friendly operating system. This is probably one of the reasons why Windows and Mac became so popular, because they were much easier to work with. However, nowadays Linux has become just as friendly with its new users.

In this chapter you will learn the basics of using Linux and using the command line terminal to get around.

Getting Started

When you work with the Raspberry Pi, you need to use the command line terminal. You already performed some very basic tasks, but there is so much more you can do through it.

When you open the terminal window, by default, you are in the home directory. With the right commands, you can navigate the entire file system and access or modify anything you want. Through the terminal you will have full administrative control over the computer, and knowing how to issue commands is important to form a solid foundation for using the Pi.

Understanding the File System

The file and folder system is fairly similar to that of any computer. A file comes in the form of video, text, or any other type of information, and you recognize it based on the name and location. Keep in mind that names are case sensitive, which means that the file Book.txt is different from BOOK.txt or bOOk.txt.

Linux stores all the files into a single root folder which you recognize by the symbol /. Within the root folder, you find subfolders which can contain more subfolders of their own and so on. An example of a root subfolder is dev/, which identifies the folder with the name "dev" in the root directory which is marked by the / symbol. You are free to make any modifications to these files and folders as long as you have the right user permission. There is only one user who can delete or modify system files, and that's marked as the "root user." You can designate as many other users as you want, but they won't have the power to change crucial system files. To avoid any unfortunate accidents, you should never stay logged in as a root user, unless you need to perform an operation that requires that level of administrative rights. Create a regular user account or several if more people need to access your computer.

You can, however, issue commands as a root user without relogging in. That is what the "sudo" command is for. It means "super user do" and when you enter it, the terminal will ask you for the root user password before it can accept your command. This shortcut can come in handy, however, you need to be sure of the command you are giving. Why? Because when you issue a "sudo" instruction, the computer won't ask you if you are really sure about it.

Basic Commands

To navigate by using the command terminal, you should know some basic commands. Many of these you will use on a daily basis, so let's see what they are and what they do.

1. **ls**: Use this command to list any files found in the directory you are currently in. You can also add a -l and type in the command like *ls -l* in order to see the file permission for each file in the list.

2. **cd**: This is used to change directory. If you issue only this command, you will be taken to the system's root directory. If you type a directory name after the command, you will be taken to that directory.

3. **sudo**: Issue a command as a root user.

4. **./filename**: Run an executable program with the specified filename. Keep in mind you need to have the right user permission to run certain programs.

5. **rm filename**: This is used to remove "filename". However, this is a permanent action. You won't be able to recover the file once you delete it.

6. **date**: If you want to know the date and time on the system, type this command.

7. **cat filename**: Read the content of a file without actually accessing it. This command is used as a sort of preview. If you aren't sure about a file and you don't want to open it inside an editor, then issue this instruction. Keep in mind that this is best used for files with text-based information in them. If you use it on an image of some kind, you will just read nonsense.

8. **pwd**: So you went on exploring through a maze of folders, and now you aren't sure where you are. Type this in and the console will display your current location.

9. **mkdir** and **rmdir**: These commands are used to create and delete a directory. For "rmdir" to work, however, you need to have an empty directory, otherwise it won't be deleted. To delete a directory with files inside it, you need to type **rmdir -p** followed by directory name.

10. **mv oldfilename newfilename**: The "mv" command is used to rename a file and destroy the old version. For example, *mv thisoldfile.txt thisnewfile.txt* renames the file "thisoldfile.txt" to "thisnewfile.txt". With this command, you can also move the new, renamed file to a new location. For example, the instruction *mv thisoldfile.txt ../MyFiles/thisnewfile.txt* will copy "thisoldfile" to the folder "MiFiles" under the new name "thisnewfile" and destroy the old version in the process.

11. **cp filename**: The "cp" command is used to make a copy of a file either in the same location, or in a new specified location. For example, if you want to copy a file from your desktop to a new location, the instruction will look like this *cp thisfile.txt ../MyFiles/thisfile.txt*.

12. **man**: This command is extremely useful when you want to know what a specific command does and what parameters it can use. Type *man command* and a manual page will open with information about that command line. You will find a description of the command, all its options, and what each option does. When viewing a manual page you can use

Enter to scroll through the text, and you return to the command terminal with Q.

13. **grep**: This command enables a search program that allows you to search through all files and folders. For instance, by typing *grep butter shoppinglist.txt* the program will look through the "shoppinglist" file for any line that contains the word "butter". The "grep" command is extremely powerful, as well as complex, but for now you only need to know its basic utility.

14. **exit**: This command is fairly self-explanatory. It is used to halt any operation that is working in the terminal, and it also closes the console.

Learning without practice is difficult, especially when it comes to memorizing commands and their uses. So open the terminal, and with a bit of creativity start using the commands listed above. Create a new directory, rename it and move it, copy it in a different location and so on.

Linux Shells

In Linux, the shell is a command line user interface. That text line terminal you have been playing with so far is also known as a shell, and Linux actually has several types. A shell is what allows you, the user, to come in contact with the system and give it direct commands. The shell you've been using so far is the "Bourne-again shell," also known as "bash," but there are others as well, such as the Korn shell, or the C shell. They all have their advantages and disadvantages, but it doesn't really matter which one you use. In this book we'll focus on the "bash" shell because that's the standard one that comes with the Raspberry Pi's Raspbian system.

So why are we talking about shells? Because each one of them comes with a different set of keyboard shortcuts that are extremely handy when you work with the terminal. Here are some of the most useful "bash" keyboard shortcuts:

1. Ctrl + A: Move the cursor to the start of the line. You can also press the "Home" button instead.

2. Ctrl + C: Kill a process that is currently running.

3. Ctrl + D: This shortcut is the same as typing "exit" in the terminal. It will close the shell.

4. Ctrl + E: Move the cursor to the end of the line. You can also press the "End" button instead.

5. Ctrl + H: Delete a character that is in front of the cursor.

6. Ctrl + L: Clear the terminal.

7. Ctrl + R: Search through the command history.

8. Ctrl + Z: Kill a program.

9. Alt + D: Delete everything after the cursor in the current line.

10. Tab: Automatic completion. When you type a command line or a file name, you can hit the "tab" button to autocomplete. When you are in the middle of a name or command and hit "tab" you may receive a list of possible commands because of similar words.

Practice these shortcuts while doing more command line exercises. Knowing them will significantly decrease the amount of time you spend typing or searching through files.

Package Management

Linux uses a package manager to manage the download, installation, configuration, and removal of software. If you've only used Windows or Mac until now, you know that installation is usually a straightforward double click on an .exe or .dmg file. Linux, however, with a package manager, will keep a record of all the installed programs and their dependencies through an internal database. This might sound a bit scary at first, but in fact it's very simple. Are you perhaps familiar with Steam, the game distribution platform? Their interface is similar to a Linux package manager.

Package managers usually have both a graphical user interface as well as a command line interface. The Raspberry Pi uses the "Aptitude" package manager, and with this computer you will probably use the command line interface most of the time.

So how do you install a program? Simple! Open the terminal and type:

```
sudo apt-get install PackageName
```

The package manager will analyze and determine what dependencies are needed for the software, download and install those dependencies, and then install the program you requested.

Text Editors and IDE's

In the same way Windows and Mac come with basic, lightweight text editors such as Notepad or Textedit, your Raspberry Pi comes with Leafpad or Nano. These editors may suffice in the beginning, but they are too lightweight when it comes to any serious programming that you will eventually have to do. The Leafpad and Nano are intuitive and easy to use, but you should switch to "Vim" or "Emacs," because they are so much more than just simple text editors. They are used as Integrated Development Environments, or IDEs, which means they provide all the tools needed by computer programmers.

Both come with in-built commands, keyword highlighting, and automatic word completion. Learning how to program is much easier when working in a proper IDE that can highlight errors, offer suggestions, and auto complete commands you are typing. Both IDE's come with pros and cons, but you can't really say one is better than the other. However, entire communities built themselves around these two programs, and they constantly argue about which one is the best. Just like with Windows vs. Mac, it's all about preference. So give both of these a try and find out what you prefer while learning. In the end, they are both tools that accomplish the same thing.

Vim

Vim is a modal editor, which means you have an "insert" mode and a "normal" mode. A basic text editor like Notepad, for instance, is considered modeless because it only has one mode where you input text. In Vim's insert mode, you input text in the editor and you commit it to the document, while normal mode is used for performing functions such as copying and pasting text or moving the cursor. This type of modal editor comes from the days when a mouse wasn't used or even needed to work on a computer. It was all about being fast and efficient with a keyboard only. Vim is a survivor of that age, and many Linux programmers prefer it to this day. But enough about tech history.

Most Raspberry Pi's already come with a version of Vim preinstalled, so let's open a text file by typing:

```
vim newfile.txt
```

Once you input the command, Vim will start in the terminal instead of a new window as you are probably used to. By default it opens in Normal mode, and you can't start editing the new file right away. You need to switch to Insert mode by typing "i". On the bottom left of the window, you will now notice the word "INSERT" showing you which mode you are in. While in this mode, you can start typing anything you want. Then you can switch back to Normal mode by hitting the "Esc" key. In both modes, you can navigate with your keyboard's arrow keys.

So you typed something in Insert mode and now you're back to Normal mode. It's time to save your file, but how? Again, make sure you are in Normal mode and type ":w", then hit the Enter key. If you want to save and exit the file at the same time, type ":x". If nothing happens, and you're just printing these symbols in the file, it means you are still in Insert mode. Always double check. Using a modal editor may take some getting used to.

Emacs

This editor has a more intuitive design than Vim and it is not modal. Keep in mind that your Raspberry Pi might not have Emacs already installed, so you have to set it up yourself. Make sure you have enough memory, because the download is somewhat large and the installation can take time due to software dependencies.

Once you have installed it, open up your terminal and type:

```
emacs newfile.txt
```

Emacs will create and open the file in a new panel, and you can start working immediately. Like previously mentioned, this is not a modal editor, so you can type whatever you want and then issue commands with keyboard shortcuts.

Here are some basic Emacs commands to get you started:

1. Ctrl + X + Ctrl + S: Save file

2. Ctrl + W: Cut

3. Alt + W: Copy

4. Ctrl + Y: Paste

5. Ctrl + X + Ctrl + C: Close file

6. Ctrl + A: Go to the beginning of line

7. Ctrl + E: Go to the end of line

8. Ctrl + Space: Set the beginning point where you will copy or cut text. You can then move the cursor to extend that selection to include the text you want.

If you aren't too comfortable with keyboard shortcut commands, Emacs has a menu where you can select what you want.

Nano

If you find Emacs and Vim a bit too challenging, you might like Nano instead. Open your terminal and type:

```
nano newfile.txt
```

Nano will create this file, or if it already exists, it will open it instead. Nano's panel is slightly different from the other two editors. The basic commands are listed at the bottom of the terminal. Type something in the file, and then save and close it. To achieve this, type "Ctrl + X" to close the program. Don't worry, it will first ask you if you want to save it. Type "y" and your test file will be saved. Explore the basic commands on your own, and try them out.

Leafpad

This is a graphical user interface-based editor that you get with your Pi. To start the program, click on the lower left icon on the desktop, go to "Accessories," and there you will find Leafpad. You will notice that this text editor is similar to Notepad. Keep in mind that this editor can only be used if you are running your computer with the graphical desktop and not the command terminal. Leafpad can't be accessed through the command line interface.

Solidify Your Linux Foundation

In this chapter you gained a basic understanding of the operating system. You learned how to use the command line interface, or the terminal, and navigate through it with basic commands. You also learned about the text editors you will need when you start programming. Explore all of them, practice with the commands, get a feel for the interface of each program, and decide which one is best suited for you.

Do you like the modal editor? Great! Look deeper into it, find some tutorials online, and learn more. Do you find it confusing and awkward? No problem, go with Emacs or one of the simpler editors instead. There is no best editor - they all are just tools at your disposal.

Chapter 3

Networking

❊ ⸱ ❊ ⸱ ❊ ⸱ ❊ ⸱ ❊ ⸱ ❊ ⸱ ❊ ⸱ ❊ ⸱ ❊ ⸱ ❊ ⸱ ❊ ⸱ ❊ ⸱ ❊ ⸱ ❊ ⸱ ❊

Networking is vital for many Raspberry Pi projects, such as home automation, and being directly connected to the Internet can also make your learning process a bit easier. The Pi can be connected to the Internet through the Ethernet port, or by connecting a USB WiFi module. The biggest benefit of a network connection, however, is probably the ability to have remote access to your Pi from another computer. If you aren't entirely comfortable with the Pi, or you don't want to connect a monitor and keyboard to it, you can simply work with it remotely from your main computer or laptop.

In this chapter we'll discuss connecting your Pi to the Internet and how to control it through the power of networking. You will learn how to set up a wireless connection, how to control your Pi remotely, how to share files through a network, how to share the screen, and more. Make sure to practice all these steps to solidify your knowledge of basic networking. You will need this information later when you work on various Pi projects.

Connecting

If you want to connect your Pi directly, you can use any Ethernet cable and connect to your router. Normally you should connect immediately, however, depending on your model and setup, you may encounter some possible issues. Most Raspbian versions are already preconfigured to establish a connection though the Dynamic Host Configuration Protocol, or DHCP. However, if your Pi's network LED doesn't blink, you might have to check your DHCP. Open up your network management panel and make sure your DHCP server is enabled.

You can also connect wirelessly with an adapter by going through your Pi's WiFi configuration tool. Simply open the program and hit the scan button to look for an access point. Click your home access point, enter the requested password and connect to the network.

These are the basic, common ways of connecting your Pi to a network. But what if there's no connection available, but you still want to remotely control your computer? Let's see what other options you have.

Using a Console Cable

If you don't want to connect a monitor and all other peripherals to your Raspberry Pi, then you can use a console cable to connect to another computer. Here's how you should establish the connection through a console cable:

1. Take the red lead and connect it to the Pi's bottom right pin.

2. Leave one open space and connect the black lead to the GND pin.

3. Take the white lead and connect it on the left side of the black lead.

4. Take the green lead and connect it to the left of the white lead.

Now you are almost ready to establish a connection with your main computer. Switch to your Windows or Mac-based PC and install the drivers needed to recognize the cable.

If you have a Mac, you can connect by opening the console and typing the following line:

```
$ screen /dev/cu.PL2303-00001004 115200
```

Your device will connect and after you hit the Enter key, you will be asked to log in to your Raspberry Pi. Use your Pi's username and password that you set up, or the default which are "pi" as username and "raspberry" as password.

If you have a Windows PC, after installing the drivers, you will need to download and install "Putty", which is a terminal program. Once you have installed it, run it and change the connection type to "serial" and set the speed to 115200. You are also required to set the serial line to be the same one as the COM port that is used by console cable. For example, it could be COM7, but if you aren't sure, or if that doesn't work, then open up your Windows Device Manager and check. When you're successful, the terminal will open and ask you for the Raspberry Pi login information.

Remote Connection with SSH

Connecting to a remote device by using Secure Shell (SSH) is extremely common because of your ability to gain encrypted access. The only drawback of using this remote connection method is the lack of a graphical user interface. So keep in mind that with SSH, you will communicate with your Raspberry Pi only through the command line interface. With that in mind, let's learn how to set it up.

Launch your Pi's configuration tool, raspi_config and enable the SSH option. It might already be enabled because some of the newest versions of Raspbian come with this function already turned on. Now switch to your main computer, and if it's a Mac, open the console and type:

```
$ ssh root@Ipaddress
```

The IP address is the IP of your Raspberry Pi. Then enter the password, and you're connected.

To connect from a Windows PC, you need to perform the same steps, but through Putty which we already discussed in the "Using a Console Cable" section.

Remote Connection with VNC

If you want to access your Pi's graphical desktop instead of the command line terminal, you need a Virtual Network Connection server. Open your console and type these commands:

```
$ sudo apt-get update
$ sudo apt-get install tightvncserver
```

This will install the VNC server to your device. Once it's installed, you need to run the server by typing:

```
$ vncserver :1
```

When you run the VNC server for the first time, you need to set up a password, which you will later use when connecting remotely from your main computer or laptop. Once you set the password, you need to switch to your Mac or PC and install the VNC client.

There are several options, but the one that is probably the most commonly used is RealVNC.

Next up, start the client and enter the IP address of your Raspberry Pi, followed by ":1". The ":1" command translates to "connect to display number 1". Now you will have to input the password you set up earlier for your VNC server.

File Sharing

The option of moving files from your Raspberry Pi to your Mac or PC and vice versa can significantly ease your work, especially if you don't have a spare keyboard and monitor. With file sharing capability, you can even access your Mac's TextMate editor from your Pi. The steps you need to take to enable file sharing are extremely similar for both Mac and PC, so we'll stick to one general explanation.

You need your computer to be able to find the Pi in the file manager application. If you're on a Mac, your Pi should show up in the Finder, and if you're using a PC, the Pi should appear in File Explorer. When you first make the connection, the device might not be visible because it requires some configuration.

First, install netatalk on your Raspberry Pi by opening the terminal and typing the following command:

```
$ sudo apt-get install netatalk
```

Now switch to your Mac and in the Finder menu click on "Connect to Server" and type afp://IPaddress as server address. Instead of IPaddress, you need to input your Pi's own IP address. Connect and log in using the Pi's default user and password. You should now be able to see the root directory of your Pi on your computer.

Network Attached Storage

In this section, you'll learn how to turn your Raspberry Pi into a file based storage platform that allows other computers to have access to shared storage. To achieve this, you first need to install Samba, a program that will help your non-Linux computer coexist with the Raspberry Pi in the same network. To start installing this software, open your terminal and type:

```
$ sudo apt-get install samba
$ sudo apt-get install samba-common-bin
```

Then connect a flash drive to your Pi. It will be automatically recognized and mounted. All you need to do now is configure Samba so that you can share the flash drive with every other computer on the network. Start by adding the default Pi user to Samba and the password. Type:

```
$ sudo smbpasswd -1 pi
```

New SMB password:

Retype new SMB password:

```
Added user pi.
```

Next you need to make some file changes. Type:

```
$ sudo nano /etc/samba/smb.conf
```

If you are going to connect a Windows PC, you need to make a change workgroup = WORKGROUP. What you need here is the workgroup name of your Windows network. For instance, on most versions of Windows nowadays, the default name is HOME. Just to be sure, check your computer first.

Next you need to find the line "# security = user" and remove the "#" symbol. By doing this, you will turn the security on.

Now go to the end of the file and type:

```
[USB]
path = /media/NAS
comment = NAS Drive
valid users = pi
writeable = yes
browseable = yes
create mask = 0777
public = yes
```

Save this file and restart the program by typing:

```
$ sudo /etc/init.d/samba restart
```

Your flash drive should now be shared with your network.

If you are connecting from a Mac, go to the Finder menu, connect to server, and type smb://rasperrypi/USB. You will then see a login window where you enter your username and password.

This operation is similar on Windows, though it can vary depending on the version you have. The only real difference from the Mac connection is that you will need to enter the network address like so: \\raspberrypi\USB and then log in with your user and password.

Chapter 4

Programming Basics Using Python

❀ ❀ ❀ ❀ ❀ ❀ ❀ ❀ ❀ ❀ ❀ ❀ ❀ ❀ ❀

As we discussed in the first chapter, the main purpose of the Raspberry Pi is to make the programming learning process more accessible and affordable to the new generations of programmers. Starting out your journey in the tech industry doesn't need to break your budget, especially if you're just exploring the world of programming and not yet committing yourself to it.

The creators who are behind the Raspberry Pi decided that programming would also be easier to understand and more entertaining if they launched their computer with the Python programming language. This language was chosen because it is considered to be extremely beginner friendly, but also powerful at the same time. Many people of all ages are picking up programming because Python makes it so easy to understand all the concepts behind this skill.

So far you have learned what makes the Raspberry Pi tick. You know how to issue commands and instructions by using the terminal, and you have a basic understanding of networking and establishing connections between devices. Now is the time to take the next step, which is a major one. You will learn the basics of programming and how to write a few basics scripts in Python. You don't need any tech knowledge to dive into this chapter. Just make sure to bring enthusiasm and an eagerness to learn, and it will all be a breeze. Also keep in mind that you should practice along with reading. You cannot learn how to program in any language without actual practice. Read, learn, understand, and put it to use.

What's Python?

Python is a general purpose programming language. Some argue that it's a scripting language and not a "real" programming language. There's no point in arguing semantics. However, you should understand the differences between the two types, what they are and what they aren't.

Programming languages, such as C, C++ or Java, are compiled languages. This means that a compiler turns the program into machine language before running it. Machine code can only be read by the computer, and most of the time programs run faster because of this process. Compilation happens only once, and the process optimizes the code for the computer to read it faster. Another key aspect is that compiled languages run directly on the machine's processor. So the code you write in C++ is run on the hardware.

Scripting languages, however, are also known as interpreted languages. They do not compile. The computer reads the code exactly as you write it, and because of this you might end up with slower programs. Keep in mind that this is influenced by how good you are at writing optimized code. If the code is sloppy and all over the place, the program will be no different. Another key difference is that a scripting language usually runs inside other programs, which will run a compilation process.

Nowadays this line between a programming language and a scripting language is so fine that you can barely tell them apart. In the past, you would have to write a program in a compiled language if that program had to benefit from the extra speed. You couldn't always use a scripting language instead. Today, computer processors are so fast that the difference in speed between the two makes no difference. You can struggle writing a program in C, or you can write simple code in Python and achieve the exact same results. The technical difference between the two types doesn't matter anymore. That is why most refer to Python as a general purpose programming language instead of a scripting language. The only difference that matters is that a scripting language is easier to learn due to simpler syntax rules. Plus, the code is very English-like. Let's see the difference up close.

Normally, the first program of a beginner is a "Hello world!" program. This is how it would look written in C, a compiled language.

```
#include <stdio.h>
int main()
{
Printf("Hello world!/n";
Return o;
}
```

Now let's see how the same program looks in Python:

```
print ("Hello world!")
```

As you can see, the Python version is a lot simpler because the code is so easy to read and understand. It's just English. While in the C version of it, you need to understand what "stdio.h" means and you need to use appropriate symbols or the program won't compile. This simplicity is why beginner programmers are directed towards Python. You will learn the same rules and concepts of programming, but with a lot less frustration that may otherwise make you give up. The creators of the Raspberry Pi knew this, and this why this computer comes with Python pre-installed. So let's get started!

Running Python

There are three methods to run Python on your Raspberry Pi. You can use IDLE, which is an integrated development environment that you should already have with your version of Linux. The other two options you have are running Python through the terminal that you are familiar with, or as a script. We'll discuss all three methods and show you how to run Python.

IDLE

This is the most user friendly way of working with Python code. Double click on the IDLE icon on your desktop. This will open a panel where you can start writing some code. As mentioned earlier, writing a "Hello, world" program is a long standing tradition in the world of programming. So let's start with that and discuss things in more detail.

Type:

```
print ("Hello, world!")
```

And hit the Enter key. You should already see the result on your screen, which is a "Hello, world!" message.

"Print" is a statement which outputs something to your screen. Let's explore this a bit further.

Type:

```
y = 7
```

Hit the enter key. There will be no output, but the program now knows that "y" is 7. Now type:

```
print (y)
```

You will be greeted with 7 as a result. What if you don't type the print statement though? Try it, type: y

You will still get 7 as a result. But why? This is called dynamic typing and it's one of the things that makes Python so easy to work with.

In a compiled language, you would have to type "int y = 7;" because you need to define the type of the variable before you declare it. The "int" tells the program that y is an integer. However, Python knows it's an integer without defining the variable, because telling it "y = 7" automatically shows that y is an integer. Before digging deeper into data types and object oriented programming, let's do a few more basic operations.

Type:

```
print (y + 3)
```

This statement will take the previous value of y, which was declared to be 7, and output 10, which is the result of 7 + 3.

Now try typing:

```
y + "home"
```

This will result in an error, however, type:

```
"welcome" + "home"
```

And you get "welcomehome" as a result. This is called string concatenation, which means that you are combining character strings together.

Now let's explore using the terminal instead of IDLE.

Using the Terminal

Start up your Pi's terminal and type "Python". You will notice that the console will display the exact same text as IDLE. The terminal will in fact work in the same way as IDLE, though it's not so pretty to look at. Try using similar commands to those discussed in the previous section. You should get the same results with the same code.

Using Scripts

You may have noticed that you cannot save the code you write in IDLE or in the terminal. You cannot write a script because when you close the panels, your code is wiped. This is why you need a text editor. With Leafpad, for instance, you write a full program, save it, and run it from the terminal. We're going to create a script using Leafpad because it's the default editor that comes with the Pi. Run the editor and let's type:

```
x = 10
y = x - 3
print (y)
```

Now save this script on your Desktop as mytest.py. Open the terminal and navigate to your desktop by typing "cd ~/desktop". You can run your new program by typing "python mytest.py". You should now see the result of your code, which in our case would be "7". Congratulation on writing your very first script, saving it, and running it successfully!

Keep in mind you can use any text editor you want to write scripts. As we already discussed, there's no better or worse editor, it's all about personal preference. If you want to stick to Leafpad, go ahead!

Now let's switch back to talking more about Python and its data types.

Python Data Types

Python comes with a few in-built data types that you should know. Learning about data types is essential for building a solid

46

programming foundation. Make sure to also keep practicing what you learn as you read along. Play with the data types you learn and with the various operations you performed until now. Don't be afraid to experiment.

Some of the most important data types are numbers, strings, dictionaries, lists, tuples and more. In this section of the chapter, we'll discuss each data type separately. Let's dive in!

Numbers

This is self-explanatory, however, there are several types of numbers. There are integers, floats, longs, complex numbers, and more. The ones you should focus on for now are integers and floats. These are the most commonly used, especially by a beginner programmer.

An integer (int in programming language) is a positive or negative whole number, so no decimal points. A float is a real number with a decimal point.

With Python, you have operators that allows you to make calculations with these numbers. Some operators such as + and - you already used, but you also have *, /, and %. There are also operators for comparison, and some of these are >, <, >=, != and more. These are basic and they're built into Python, however there are many more that can only be used by importing a module.

What's a Python module? A module is an extra library that you import to your script so that you can add to the functionality of the programming language. In the case of numbers, you might want to perform some fancier mathematical functions, so you'll need to import the "math" module. Let's see how this works in action. Open a new IDLE panel and type:

```
a = -6.02
print abs(a)
```

You will get the result without a problem because the absolute value function is already included in native Python. We'll talk more about functions a bit later. Now type:

```
ceil (15.4)
```

You will see an error because the native library does not contain the ceiling function. You need to import it first, so let's import the math module. Type:

```
import math
math.ceil(15.4)
```

Now you will get the result, which in this case is 16. Even if you don't need the ceiling function, or you don't know what it is yet, having this module imported is useful for performing trigonometric functions and so much more. If you want to play more with numbers and calculations, go ahead. Discover things on your own and have fun while exploring!

Strings

A string is a sequence of characters, or in other words, it's text. Strings can be anything that simply gives you text-based information. This includes letters, names, punctuation marks, and even numbers. Didn't we just say numbers are a separate data type? Yes we did, it's all about the way you type the code. Here's an example:

```
y = 20 and y = "20"
```

The difference may be subtle, but with the first version of the code you can make mathematical calculations. With the second version, you will get an error. Because the number 20 is enclosed in quotes, the program sees it as a string. Without the quotes, it's an integer.

So what can you do with strings? A lot, but let's see some of the basic operations, such as determining the length of a string, concatenation, and iteration.

Let's open a new IDLE panel and type:

```
len("welcome")
```

Len is used to determine the length of a string, therefore the result will be 7, because the word "welcome" is made of 7 characters. Now try:

49

```
'cats' + 'and' + 'dogs'
```

This is an example of string concatenation that we discussed a bit earlier. The result will be catsanddogs, but that's not readable. Why aren't there any spaces between words? Because we didn't add the space. Try this instead:

```
'cats ' + 'and ' + 'dogs'
```

Now the result will be "cats and dogs". Did you notice anything else with the last two lines of code? We switched from double quotes to single quotes and everything worked just fine. That's because Python doesn't tell the difference between the two, so you can use whichever symbol you prefer.

Let's see how to iterate every character in a string. Type:

```
booktitle = "Lord of the Rings"
for c in booktitle: print c,
...
```

This will print every character within booktitle "Lord of the Rings".

There are many more string operations that you can perform. You can convert words to ASCII code, uppercase to lowercase, and much more. For now, it's enough if you understand what strings are and how to use them. You are free to explore more on your own.

Python's string library is extensive, and there are modules you can import as well.

Lists

A list is a very important and useful data type frequently used in programming. They can always be changed, they can contain different types of objects, you can increase or reduce their size, and much more. If you are familiar with a C derived programming language, you will notice that Python lists are actually arrays. Everything you can do with strings, you can also do with lists. Let's see how to create one. Type:

```
x = [1, 2, 3, 4, 5, 6, 7, 8, 9, 10]
```

As you can see, lists are declared by using square brackets []. Now type:

```
book = ["title", 1, 2, 3, "42"]
```

Now feel free to play with the exact operation you learned in the string sections. Here's how a concatenation would look like:

```
x + book
```

The result will be a concatenation of the two lists, so you will see:

```
[1, 2, 3, 4, 5, 6, 7, 8, 9, 10, "title", 1, 2, 3, "42"]
```

Experiment with other operations and see what happens!

If you are confused by a certain data type, you can ask Python for advice. For example type:

```
import string
help (string)
```

Python will tell you everything you want to know about strings.

Dictionaries

These are flexible collections of objects just like lists, except they aren't ordered. To have access to an item in a dictionary, you will need to access it by a key. When you request the key, you will receive the object associated with it. Let's see an example. Type:

```
dict = {'fruit' : 'apple', 'vegetable' : potato'}
dict ['vegetable']
```

The printed result will be "potato". Keep in mind that the key doesn't have to be a string like "vegetable", it can also be an integer or other objects.

Tuples

Tuples are sequences of objects that cannot be changed. They are similar to lists because you can order them, but you can't change them once they are in place. Let's see how a tuple looks like by typing:

```
t = (0, 2, 'something', 42, [1, 2, 3])
```

As you might've noticed, the tuple is written with parentheses. In our line of code we have a tuple that contains three integers, a string, and a list. You can perform any operation you tried on lists in previous section. They are nearly identical to lists. The only difference is that once you've declared a sequence of integers, strings, lists or any other objects as a tuple, you cannot later change anything further in your program. If you try to make a change to the tuple, you will receive an error. It's similar to declaring a constant in C, or C++ if you are familiar with programs in the C family.

Now that you know the basics of the most important data types, you can put your knowledge to the test.

Python Programming

Let's make an actual program now that you know about data types and basic operators. If you were using an interpreter so far, now you need to switch to a text editor like Leafpad or Emacs. Open the editor, and save it immediately as a file with the .py extension. You

53

will then be able to run the program by typing $ python thisprogram.py, as we mentioned earlier in the chapter.

First, let's discuss the block structure of the code. Python is somewhat special in the world of programming languages because it splits out code by using whitespace blocks. Most languages split the code into blocks by starting and ending with curly braces. Here's an example of a code block written in C:

```c
if (y == 10)
{
    printf ("y is equal to ten");
    printf ("Nothing else to do here");
}
printf ("This is the end of the if statement");
```

Now let's write the same if statement in Python:

```python
if y == 10 :
    print ("y is equal to ten")
    print ("Nothing else to do here")
print ("This is the end of the if statement")
```

It's worth mentioning that in Python the parentheses are optional, however, using them is considered a standard in programming. The code is considered to be more readable this way, therefore it's a standard to use parentheses even in Python. The above if statement written in C has the obligatory parentheses. The same if statement in Python is written without the parentheses, however, you should use them anyway. Getting used to best practices will also help you if you ever wish to learn a C programming language.

Did you also notice any other important difference between the two blocks of code? In C, C++ or C#, you need to end lines of code with a semicolon ";". If you don't, the code will not compile and the program won't work. In Python, there is no need for the semicolon. A line of code ends simply at the end of the line.

Naming Conventions

Before we move on to learn more about statements, you should familiarize yourself with variable naming conventions to keep your code clean, readable, and consistent. When you start learning programming, you need to know how to organize your project. You may write the code only once, but chances are it will be read several times and not always by you. If you don't use an easy to understand naming convention, other programmers will have a hard time reading your code. Even you will struggle after a few days or weeks of not working on your project. A program is supposed to explain itself to the coder, so naming things properly is extremely important. Let's discuss the several naming conventions that are well known.

1. **Pascal Case**: Capitalize the first letter of every word and don't leave any empty spaces or symbols between the words. Pascal case looks like this: ThisIsPascalCase, UserAccount, FileName.

2. **Camel Case**: This is very similar to Pascal case. The only difference is that the first word starts with a lowercase letter. For example: thisIsCamelCase, userInterface, combatSystem.

3. **Snake Case**: This is the method of naming variables with compound words where each word is separated by an underscore. Snake case can be written either with every first letter of every word in lowercase, or with the first letter of the first word in upper case. Don't leave any space and don't use any symbols. This is how snake case looks: this_is_snake_case, Also_snake_case, user_interface. With this naming convention, you might find it easier to read descriptive compound words because the underscore looks like a space. Snake case is also an extremely popular naming convention for project files.

4. **Apps Hungarian Notation**: The name of the variable begins with a lowercase prefix that indicates its type or intention. This naming convention was adopted by Microsoft, and it is somewhat widely used. Here are some examples: rwPosition (rw refers to a row), usName (us refers to unsafe string). This naming system may sound confusing and difficult, especially when you are a beginner programmer.

These are the most commonly used naming conventions no matter which programming language you use. There is no "best." The most important thing is consistency. Don't use several naming conventions in the same program, as you may cause confusion and make the code harder to read. Choose the one that seem to be the easiest to read for you and stick to it.

Conditional Statements

It's time to teach your program how to make decisions on its own. A conditional statement will check the condition of a variable and change the result of the program based on the value.

You might have notice that you already encountered conditionals in previous sections. The "if statement" is probably the most well-known statement, not just because of its use in programming, but because of how much we use it in real life. For instance: If it rains tomorrow, I will stay home. You can also be more specific and state what happens if it doesn't rain tomorrow. For example: If it rains tomorrow, I will skip work, else I will go for a walk. If statements and if-else statements are extremely common in programming, so let's see how they look in code. Type:

```
x = 10
if x > 10:
    print("x is a large number")
```

As you can see, we begin by declaring X's value. Then we use an "if statement" to determine whether what we declared is true. In our example we're checking if x is greater than 10. If it's true, the program will print the message "x is a large number". In programming, most of the time we also want to specify what happens if the statement is false. Type:

```
x = 10
if x > 10:
    print("x is a large number")
else:
    print("x is a small number")
print ("This message will print no matter what")
```

In this block of code, we state just like before that x is 10 and if it's larger than 10, the program should print "x is a large number". If x isn't greater than 10, the first part of the statement will be ignored and the "else" part of the statement will be printed. At the end of the statement we also added a "control" message that will be printed in both cases, no matter the result.

There is a third statement that can be added here: the "elif" statement, which is used to check multiple expressions for true and execute the code when the condition is met. Here's how the structure would look like with "elif" included.

```
if condition1:
    statements
elif condition2:
    statements
elif condition3:
    statements
```

```
else:
    statements
Here's an example with code. Type:
x = 100
if x > 200:
    print ("x is a large number")
elif x < 50:
    print ("x is a small number")
else:
    print ("x is not as huge as I thought")
```

When the code is executed, you will be greeted with the result "x is not as huge as I thought".

Conditionals are important in all programming languages, so practice them. Be creative, use integers and floats, make some simple calculations, and then use a conditional statement to test the result and output a result.

Assignment Operators

These operators are used to assign a value to a variable. Let's see some examples and explain with words what the most common assignment operators do.

```
x = 10
```

This is the most basic assignment operator, and in this example we simply assign the value of 10 to our x variable.

```
X += 10
```

The plus equal operator is the same as saying "x = x + 10". Here's a simple example of how it works:

```
X = 2
X += 5
print(x)
```

The result is 7.

The following assignment operators work in the same way as the plus equal operator. They are self-explanatory, so try them out yourself like in the example above.

```
X -= 5
x *= 5
x /= 5
```

There are other assignment operators, but for the purpose of learning basic programming in Python, we will stick to these for now. You can explore the rest if you wish by searching online for "assignment operators" or by using the Python help command as explained earlier.

Comparison Operators

Also known as relational operators, they are used to compare the value on each side of the operator and determine the relation between them. You already used a couple of basic comparison operators, but let's take a look at all of them and what they mean.

The "less than" operator: <

The "greater than" operator: >

The "less than or equal to" operator: <=

The "greater than or equal to" operator: >=

The "equal to" operator: ==

The "not equal to" operator: != or <>

Let's test all of these comparison operators. You can use the terminal for this part. Type:

10 != 100

10 is not equal to 100, therefore the statement is true.

2 != 2

2 is not equal to 2, this is false.

1 >= 1

True

Continue using the rest of the operators and check the results. Keep in mind, however, that you need to use a double equal (==) when you are comparing values. In programming, a single equal is used to set a value.

Logical Operators

This type of operator is used usually together with conditional statements because they allow you to make several comparisons in one statement. There are three logical operators: and, or, and not.

The "and" operator will return true if both statements are true.

The "or" operator will return true if one of the statements is true.

The "not" operator will reverse the result, which means it will return false if the result is true.

Let's see a logical operator in action within an "if" statement. Type:

```
x = 50
if x <= 100 and x >= 10:
    print("x is somewhere in the middle")
```

With this code, we are checking whether x's value is somewhere between 100 and 10.

Try practicing with the conditional statements you learned in the section above. You can use as many logical operators as you want, as well as conditional statements. Remember, the key to learning is practice.

Loops

Code is executed line by line, vertically from top to bottom. Normally, a line of code is executed only once, followed by the next line, and the next, and so on. There are, however, cases when we want a block of code to repeat until a certain condition is met. In Python, you will use two kinds of loops, namely "for" loops and "while" loops. Let's see some examples to get a better understanding. We'll start with the for loops. Type:

```
for x in range(1, 10):
print(x)
```

What happens here? The program will repeat the command to iterate over a range. In this case, the for loop is used to repeat a block of code a certain number of times defined by the range function. Let's see another example by typing the following:

```
vegetables = ["potatoes", "cucumbers", "cabbages",
"carrots"]
for x in vegetables:
    print(x)
```

In this block of code we create a list of vegetables, and with the use of a for loop we can print each item in the list. Now let's see how to loop through a string. Type:

```
for x in "Python";
    print(x);
```

In this case, the for loop is printing each character contained in the string. Strings are iterable objects, because they are a sequence of characters.

What if you want to repeat a block of code only while a certain condition is met? The key word in that question is "while". A "while" loop is used to run a part of the program until a variable changes. Let's see a simple demonstration:

```
x = 1
while x <= 5:
    print(x)
    x += 1
```

Let's break down this block of code. We assign the value of 1 to x. Then we state that while the value of x is smaller than or equal to 5, the program should print x. At this stage, if we end the block of code, we will create an endless loop that will print 1 as the value of x, because that's what we told the program to do so far. What we want is to use an assignment operator to tell the program to repeat the code only until the condition is no longer met. Therefore, when x reaches 5, the loop ends, because we told the program to execute only as long as x is smaller than or equal to 5.

Congratulations! You now know how to write loops in Python. But what happens if the condition of the loop is always true, and it never changes? You can end up with an infinite loop, and that's bad. In this case, you can use a "break" statement to break out of the loop. Here's an example of a loop break:

```
while True:
    response = input("Enter command:")
    if response == "Y":
        break
```

This block of code will continue asking you to enter to correct response. The loop will only break when you give the program what it asks for. Try it out. If you enter any command other than uppercase Y, the program will keep telling you to "enter command". Typing "Y" is the only way to exit the loop.

Take note that this block of code might not work in your version of Python. The "input" command is used in Python 3. If you are working in Python 2 by any chance, replace the command with "raw_input".

Practice Python's primary loops by using everything else you learned in the previous chapters. Loops are part of basic programming, and understanding them is crucial. "For" and

"While" loops are concepts used in all programming languages, and they are needed in many projects. Use the information you acquired so far to make simple programs. However, if you are feeling a little overwhelmed, look up Python loop exercises online instead.

Functions

When you're programming, you don't want to repeat the same code several times in your program. This is what functions are for. They allow you to be more efficient and avoid reusing the same code. Generally, it is considered that if you need to write the same code more than twice, you should use a function. This is not a rule by any means, but many programmers within the industry consider this to be best practice.

Here's a simple example of how to create a function:

```
def friendly_function():
    print("Function says hello!")
```

We define a faction by using the keyword "def". Don't forget to pay attention to your chosen naming convention. We use the same conventions as for variables. In this example we used Snake Case.

Now that we have the function defined, we need to call it. Type the name of your function, followed by parentheses:

```
friendly_function()
```

When you call it, the program will print the message "Function says hello!".

What are the parentheses for, you ask? Functions can be used to pass information as a parameter. A parameter is a variable that is given in the definition of the function. Here's an example of a function with parameters:

```
def my_name(firstname):
    print(firstname + " Smith")
my_name("John")
my_name("James")
my_name("Andrew")
```

In the "my_name" function we determine one parameter, which is "firstname". Then we call the function to print out the parameter within it, which is any first name, in order to display the full name. Keep in mind that this is just a basic example. Functions aren't limited to one parameter. You can have no parameters, one parameter, or as many as you want. If you use multiple parameters, however, make sure to separate them with a comma.

Now that you understand how functions work and what parameters are, let's see how to use a default parameter. What does that even mean? If you establish a function with a default parameter value, you can call the function without a parameter because it will use the default value you gave it. Let's see this concept in action. Type:

```
def your_function(country = "Germany"):
    print ("I am from " + country)
your_function("China")
your_function("France")
your_function()
your_function("Italy")
```

The result should look something like this:

```
I am from China
I am from France
I am from Germany
I am from Italy
```

As you can see, if you define a default parameter and you don't mention the parameter during a function call, you will print with the default value, in our case "I am from Germany".

All the functions we listed so far are simply doing something. They do not return any value. If you want your function to return a value, you have to use the return command. When the function returns a value, you can assign it to a variable. Here's an example:

```
def your_function(x):
    return 10 * x
print(your_function(2))
print(your_function(5))
```

In this case, you return a new value and you print it.

Continue practicing functions by creating your own exercises. You can establish any kind of parameter, so use your knowledge of lists and other variable types to understand the power of functions.

Commenting Your Code

Increasing the readability of your code is one of your priorities when programming. So far we discussed the importance of variables, function naming conventions, and organizing your code, but there's one extra step you can take. A programmer needs to make the code understandable, not only to himself, but to others as well. The way to achieve this is by using comments. Even if you work alone on your project, you might take a break at some point and return to it later. What happens? The code you wrote isn't so fresh and familiar anymore. You struggle to understand what you really tried to do. Code commenting is a way to offer explanations that can shed light on a complex block of code.

Keep in mind that comments are meant for the programmers who read the code. They don't affect the program itself in any way. Here's how to write a comment in Python:

```
# This is a comment
```

The comment itself is marked with a # symbol. The program will ignore everything that is written after a hash mark. You can place a comment wherever you want, even inside a line of code, and it won't interfere with the program.

print("This code will be executed") # This part will be ignored

While comments can be inserted anywhere, you should also pay attention to how you write them. You don't want an endless comment line that requires scrolling in order to read. Comments should be short, however, sometimes you need to offer a more detailed explanation. Whenever you need to write more than around 70 characters, you should consider writing a new line. Here's how you can write a multiline comment in Python:

```
# This is an example
# on how to break down
# comments into multiple lines
```

This method is involves creating a new line and adding the hash mark at the beginning of it. This is the only right way of commenting your code in Python. There is another method, but it is not considered best practice. It involves creating a block comment, wrapped in-between quotation marks, like this:

```
"""
If you don't want to add
a hash mark every single
line, you can just write the
comment like this
"""
```

Take note that the triple quote method is in fact a string that isn't assigned to a variable, and not a comment. You can use this as a comment, however, because a string like this will be completely ignored at runtime. The use of this method is risky, because if you place the triple quote block comment in the wrong place in your code, you can associate it with an object.

Learning how to comment within your code is a much needed skill, especially once your program starts to grow. It will save you a lot of time in the long run, and if you work with other programmers, you will give them fewer reasons to hate you.

Chapter 5

Advanced Programming with Python

❀ ❀ ❀ ❀ ❀ ❀ ❀ ❀ ❀ ❀ ❀ ❀ ❀ ❀ ❀

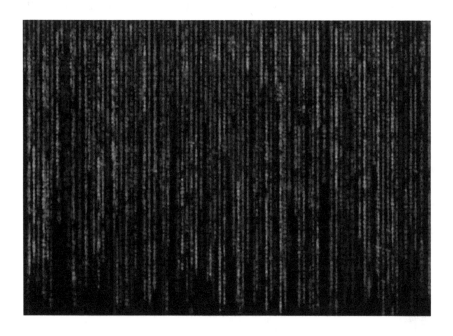

So far, you learned the most basic concepts of programming, and you had a practical introduction to working with Python. You learned about data types, operator types, naming conventions, functions, conditional statements, and you (hopefully) did a few exercises as well to solidify some of the information.

If you feel like you are struggling to understand some of the concepts, don't beat yourself up. There's a lot of knowledge to absorb, and it can be overwhelming at first. Take each chapter and each section separately. Do some exercises. Look for additional guidance online. The Python community is quite vast, and many programmers are willing to help you start on the right path. This book should be enough to get you started with programming, however, the main purpose is to teach you how to work with the Raspberry Pi and to enable you to create various projects.

In this chapter we will discuss the more advanced concepts behind Python and focus more on object-oriented programming. You will learn about classes, methods, how to handle exceptions, and more.

Some of these advanced concepts may not be needed in the project section of the book. We will only briefly discuss a few of Pythons advanced concepts to broaden your horizons. However, when we explore the use of the Raspberry Pi in real projects, you will be guided and instructed step by step. You don't have to be an expert programmer by the time you reach that part of the book, however, you should grasp the basic concepts of programming and understand what is needed from you to work on a project. Like we mentioned before, practice makes perfect, so go slowly through these sections. Read and reread, but most importantly do your best to use this information to create small blocks of code on your own. It might take some time, but your future self will be grateful when you're successfully creating cool projects. So let's get started!

Object-Oriented Programming

Python is one of the popular programming languages that supports OOP, or object-oriented programming, but what does it actually mean? OOP is a paradigm which is based on containing data in the shape of objects with attributes and methods. In this case, an object is actually a collection of data types that you already know from the previous chapter, such as integers, floats, and strings. Objects are usually generalized in classes of objects and they have associated methods that act on all members belonging to such a class.

This may sound extremely confusing and maybe even difficult to read to the uninitiated, so let's try and explain OOP through an analogy.

Let's say our class is a vehicle. A class defines attributes and behavior, so in our case, the attributes of the vehicle are model, type of fuel, color and so on. The behavior or method of the class can be start, break, accelerate, and so on. With the vehicle class, we can then create various objects that share some of these attributes and behaviors. For instance, object 1 is a Renault Clio car model that uses diesel as fuel and was made in 2014. Object 1 can start, stop, accelerate and so on. This Renault Clio object belongs to the vehicle class. Then we can create a second object with same common behavior. This way, with OOP, you can create a blueprint of the vehicle and create various objects from it. Hopefully this vehicle analogy can shed some light on this concept.

There are 4 principles of object-oriented programming that you should know, namely encapsulation, abstractions, inheritance, and polymorphism. You may not need to know these principles in details in order to make full use of this book, however, you should be aware of them at the very least.

1. **Encapsulation**: This is achieved when we place certain objects inside a private class. Other objects will not be able to access the objects within it. This principle is used to add security to the program by not giving authority to other objects to change anything about the encapsulated objects.

2. **Abstraction**: Many programs are large, making code maintenance a difficult task. This is why we apply the abstraction concept. Internal details about an object will be hidden because they are unnecessary when performing other operations. We want to reveal only the operations that are relevant for other related objects. For instance, you have a coffee machine. On the inside, the machine performs a lot of tasks you aren't aware of. However, all you need to know is that you have to press a button to get coffee.

3. **Inheritance**: This concept is used when you have many objects that are very similar, yet not identical. You can extract what they have in common and apply that logic to a new class. In programming terms, through inheritance you create a child class from the parent class. Essentially, you will form a hierarchy. The child class will reuse all the common logic found in the parent class. However, you will afterwards add the unique part that will be used only by the child class.

4. **Polymorphism**: As previously mentioned, you want to avoid duplicating code. If objects can take more than a single form, you can cut down on unnecessary code. A program can determine through context which form of an object is needed in order to execute the code. Polymorphism is a great way of maintaining your program and keeping it short and as a clean as possible.

Learning and understanding the concepts of object-oriented programing will help you in your future, more complex programs. But enough with theory for now. Let's get back to programming with Python and start coding!

String Formatting

String formatting is used for substituting variables and formatting values by concatenating elements inside the string through positional formatting. This works by leaving a placeholder in a string and then calling the formatting method. This placeholder is marked with curly brackets "{ }".

Important! There are two ways of performing string formatting, and it depends on your version of Python. If you are using Python 3, you will call the method with the "str.format()" command. This will also work in Python 2.7 because of backwards compatibility that was implemented a while ago. If you use an older version, you will have to use the % operator. We'll discuss both methods, because it's still common to use the % operator, therefore it's important for you to recognize it. Let's start with the old method:

```
name = "World"
'Hello, %s' % name
```

The result will be "Hello World". The "%s" is used as a format specifier that tells the program to substitute the value of "name" represented as a string. Here's how this code would look with the new method:

```
name = "World"
"Hello, {}" .format(name)
```

Now let's use string formatting to perform a slightly more complicated operation. Let's convert a date to a string and then format it. Type:

```
from datetime import datetime
d = datetime.now()
"{:%Y-%m-%d %H:%M:%S}".format(d)
```

This code block looks a bit like gibberish, doesn't it? That's because when it comes to formatting, there's a whole language involved. Each symbol means something. For example, %Y refers to the year, while %M refers to minutes. The result you get with this code should be the "year-month-day hour: minutes: seconds".

How to Define a Class

We discussed earlier object-oriented programming, classes, and objects. Let's see how you can define a class and declare all the variables you need. Type:

```
class Person:
    # This is a comment. Use it to explain the purpose of the
class
    def _init_(self, name, tel):
            self.name = name
            self.tel = tel
```

As was mentioned earlier, a class is a blueprint, or a template. What we did so far with the code above is just define the class. There are no objects yet. Within the class we have a constructor method declared with "_init_". This constructor will be called when you create a new instance of the "person" class.

Next up we have the keyword "self" which is absolutely necessary in Python when you define a method inside a class. In other programming languages like Java, we have the same concept, but the keyword "this" is used instead. With the line "self.name = name" we create the "name" variable that is accessible to all the other members of the same class, and we initialize it with the value passed to the call in order to create an instance. Let's test this by typing:

```
p = Person("Smith", "123321")
```

```
p.name
```

The result will be "Smith" because with this code we checked that the object "p" has the name "Smith".

How to Define a Method

In Python, a method is actually a function that belongs to an object or class. It is only used for the object for which it's called, and it's accessible only to the data that is contained in the class. Here's an example:

```
class Pet (object):
    def my_method(self):
            print ("This is a dog")
dog = Pet()
dog.my_method()
```

In this block of code we define the "Pet" class, create a "dog" object and call a method by using the object.

Inheritance

Define a class and use inheritance to create a subclass to which you can add new variables and methods. We already briefly discussed the concept behind inheritance, so let's see how you can implement it:

```
class Employee(Person)
```

```
    def _init_ (self, name, contact, salary):
            super()._init_(name, contact)
            self.salary = salary
    def give_raise(self, amount):
            self.salary = self.salary + amount
```

As you can see, we are creating a subclass called "Employee" from the "Person" class. Then we add "salary" as a new variable and a new method "give_raise" that are specific only to this subclass.

Writing to a File

In Python, you can write a file by default without importing any modules. You can use the functions open, write, and close to open a file, write to it, and close it. Here's how it looks in code:

```
f = open ("testfile.txt", "w")
f.write ("This file contains more data")
f.close()
```

When we create a file, we need to use a file mode to specify in which mode we want to open the file. In this case we use "w", which stands for "write", to specify that we want to create a new file. There are a few other file modes as well: read, append, binary, and text. You can also combine these modes together like this:

```
f = open ("testfile2.txt", "r + b")
```

Reading from a File

Similar to writing to a file, we need to use file methods in order to read from a file. Here's an example:

```
f = open("demotest.txt")
x = f.read()
f.close()
```

This code will read the content of the file into the "x" variable.

Handling Exceptions

A program will stop as soon as it comes across an error, whether it's a syntax error or an exception. However, if an exception is handled, the termination will be prevented. You may have already encountered syntax errors because they happen when making an incorrect statement. Here's an example:

```
print ("Hello world"))
SyntaxError: Invalid syntax
```

In our example we get a syntax error because of the second parenthesis we added. This is a common error, because it frequently happens due to basic mistakes such as this. They are always fatal, however, because the program won't work with present syntax errors. Luckily, these are easy to solve because the parser will repeat the line with the error and point an arrow where it detected the problem.

Handling an exception, however, is a bit trickier because the program knows what to do with code but is still incapable of performing an action. For instance, if you tell Python to connect to the Internet, but there is no actual connection, it will fail and throw you an exception. You can write your code in such a way to handle exceptions, otherwise your program will be terminated when the error is encountered.

Let's take a division by zero as an example. If you type:

```
x = 10/0
print (x)
```

You will get a ZeroDivisionError: division by zero exception. We can handle this exception by using a try and except block, which is probably the most common way of dealing with most errors of this type. How does it work? The program will execute the code after the "try" statement like a normal part of the code. Afterwards, the code following the "except" statement will be the way the program will respond to the resulting exception that occurs in the "try" section of the block. Let's take our earlier example and see how to handle its exception:

try:

```
    x = 10/0
print (x)
    except ArithmeticError:
```

```
print ("Arithmetic exception is raised")
else:
print ("It works")
Result: Arithmetic exception is raised.
```

Python Modules

As we mentioned in an earlier chapter, Python has many modules or libraries available. Some of them are included, and others need to be downloaded and installed separately. You can even import multiple modules, but be careful because there can be conflict between them. As a consequence of using too many modules at once, you can encounter a function with the same name more than once. This can lead to problems, but luckily you can choose how much of a module you can access. Here's how you import a module:

```
import random
```

This is a module for random numbers, and you won't encounter any conflicts because you will only access the functions within this module. However, if you plan to use multiple modules, but you don't need everything contained in them, you can specify the component. Type:

```
from random import randint
print(randint(1,10))
```

The component "randint" is part of the random numbers module, and in this example is used to generate a random number from 1 to 10. There are many more modules for Python, and even more components for each module. You can find all of them in Python's documentation.

Sending an Email

So why would you ever want to send an email from Python? You might work on a project which involves motion detection, like some kind of security system. For example, with Python's Simple Mail Transfer Protocol module, you can program your Pi to send out an email whenever it detects motion. Here's how you can send an email from a Gmail account.

```
import smtplib
GMAIL_USER = "your_email_address@gmail.com"
GMAIL_PASS = "your_account_password"
SMTP_SERVER = "smtp.gmail.com"
SMTP_PORT = 587
def send_email (recipient, subject, text)
smotpserver = smtplib.SMTP(SMTP_SERVER, SMTP_PORT)
smtpserver.ehlo()
smtpserver.starttols()
smtpserver.ehlo
smtpserver.login(GMAIL_USER, GMAIL_PASS)
header = "To:" + recipient + "\n" + "From: " + GMAIL_USER
header = header + "\n" + "Subject:" + subject + "\n"
msg = header + "\n" + text + " \n\n"
smtpserver.sendmail(GMAIL_USER, recipient, msg)
```

```
smtpserver.close()
send_email("your_destination_email_address", "sub", "this
is the text")
```

Use your own Gmail account information instead of GMAIL_USER and GMAIL_PASS, and don't forget to also change the destination email address. If you are using another service instead of Gmail, you will have to change SMTP_SERVER and SMTP_PORT.

Chapter 6

Electronics Basics

❅ ◦ ❅ ◦ ❅ ◦ ❅ ◦ ❅ ◦ ❅ ◦ ❅ ◦ ❅ ◦ ❅ ◦ ❅ ◦ ❅ ◦ ❅ ◦ ❅ ◦ ❅ ◦ ❅

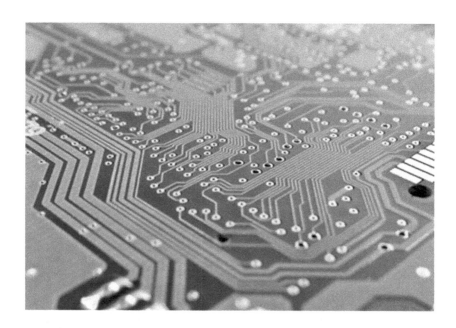

Now that you have a fundamental understanding of Python programming, it's time to take a look at electronics and basic electricity concepts. After all, we want to be able to build cool projects with the Raspberry Pi. Before you can do that, however, you need to understand the rules of electricity, the tools you'll be working with, and safety regulations. You'll be working with various electronics, and you can injure yourself if you don't receive some safety instruction.

Electricity Fundamentals

Since you'll be working with electronics and power supplies for your projects, the first thing you should learn is Ohm's law. It states that the voltage in a circuit equals the product of the current times the resistance. Let's break this down a bit. The voltage is measured in volts (V), the product of the current is referring to Inductance (I) which is measured in amps, and the resistance (R) is measured in Ohms. Therefore, if you have a 200 Ohm resistor with 0.045 amps passing through, you will have 9V (volts) across the resistor.

The second most important thing to understand when it comes to electricity is power (P). It is measured in Watts and it is equal to the voltage times current. Power will increase with current and resistance. In a way, you can look at it as the speed of electricity. You can compare it to water going through a hose. If you apply resistance to the end of the hose by using your finger, the speed of the flow will increase. In a similar fashion, you increase power by increasing the resistance. There are, however, consequences to this. When you increase the resistance, you will gain more heat as a result. Heat is the enemy of electronics, especially smaller, fragile electronic components. This is why we have heat sinks in laptops, smartphones, and tablet components.

In the simplest terms, electricity is just electrons moving back and forth along the path of least resistance. Being aware of this, you should always make sure that the easiest path doesn't involve your own body. Wearing rubber gloves, or rubber boots when the gloves are impractical, can significantly reduce your odds of being electrocuted.

Tools

You'll be working on a lot of different projects and you will certainly need a variety of tools. When working with sensitive electronics and small components, you'll want to use high quality tools that are up to the task. Whether you're a pro or a hobbyist, you shouldn't be using any old, bent, rusty screwdriver you have in some long forgotten drawer. Do not ignore the importance of a good set of tools. With that in mind, let's take a look at what you'll need for all the cool Raspberry Pi projects you'll soon be working on.

Screwdrivers

Good quality screwdrivers are crucial to anyone's robotics kit. You need a small selection of jeweler's screwdrivers made of hardened steel in order to avoid causing damage to the tip of a screw. Damaged screws can make your life hard when you're concentrating on your project, but you keep losing the grip on them.

You'll need at the very least three different sizes of both regular and Phillips screwdrivers. Regular ones should range from 1.20 millimeters (3/64'') to 3.1 millimeters (1/8''). As for Phillips screwdrivers, you are looking for #0, #1, and #2. Also make sure you have multipurpose sized screwdrivers, because you will be working with regular-sized screws when assembling parts, not just miniature ones.

Wire Cutters

Invest only in high quality cutters. Even if they're more expensive, keep in mind you are working with small electronic components that can easily be damaged by dull, low quality steel cutters.

You will need two kinds of wire cutters: one for general purpose, and one for delicate work. You will eventually have to cut small solder joints or the frayed ends of wires.

Wire Strippers and Pliers

While you might manage with standard-sized pliers you may already have lying around the house, you should get your hands on some needle-nosed pliers instead. You will handle a lot of fine, sensitive components that require precision-work. With needle-nosed pliers, you can gently bend various parts, or use them as a pair of tweezers.

When it comes to wire stripping, you might be able to improvise with the wire cutting area of your pliers, but that can be tedious, especially when you have to do it often. Invest a bit of money into wire-strippers instead, because they are built especially for this task.

Files

Working with electronics will involve a lot of soldering of wire ends. A file will be handy for preparing a joint for soldering or for removing the excess solder material from a wire. Files are also great for enlarging holes and reshaping plastic as well as metal. You don't need any fancy tools for this, just get any set of files with various degrees of roughness.

Light

As we already mentioned a few times, you will mostly be working with really tiny components that require fine, precision work. Dealing with tiny resistors and even tinier servo connections will tire your eyes and ruin your ability to focus in a matter of minutes. What you need is more light, but not just any light. What you are looking for is magnifying light.

A desk lamp with a built-in magnifier will work wonders and significantly improve your ability to work on your project. You can find these magnifying lights in stores dedicated to selling tools for jewelers and watchmakers.

Glue Gun and Glues

Not all projects involve attaching components by using screws. You're going to need a glue gun. Invest in a top notch hot glue gun!

You might be tempted by the cheaper ones found in supermarkets, but those are mainly designed for light work for school children. You won't be scrapbooking here. You'll be connecting electronic components and metal to plastic.

You'll also need a variety of glues that aren't meant for glue guns. Typically, you need at least two kinds of glue, and those are superglue and modeling cement. Rubber cement and epoxy can also come in very handy.

Speaking of sticky things, you'll also want to add tape to your shopping list. You will need electrical tape, transparent tape, double-sided tape and last but not least, duct tape.

Multimeter

This device is used for measuring the voltage, resistance, and current. You will need one of these to make sure you are using the correct voltage, learn how much resistance there is between two points in a circuit, and even trace an electrical short.

There are two types that you can get, either an analog multimeter or a digital one. The most important aspect, however, is not how many features it has, but how user-friendly it is. You can invest a lot of money into a complex multimeter, but if you aren't trained in how to use a highly specialized one, you won't use it at all.

Soldering Iron

This tool can be found just about anywhere. You can spend even $10 on one, but only get by with it in the beginning. As you progress with your projects, you will want a more versatile soldering iron.

With a cheap hobby tool you have no control over the heat and might damage the circuit board. What you need is an adjustable soldering iron. These tools come with temperature adjustment so that you can use the right amount of heat for the task. You might need to melt off a failed solder connection, and you don't want to melt the board with it. They also come with replaceable soldering heads, so that you can use thinner or thicker ones depending on the soldering joints you need.

Power Supplies

Your project will require power, and you have several options for supplying it. In most cases you will get by with only using batteries. It simply depends on each project's requirements. The most important item you'll need is probably an adjustable AC/DC power convertor that you can find in any electronics store. The most common voltage source you'll need will be 9V and 12V with various current ratings.

Breadboard

No, not the literal bread board you use to slice your bread. A breadboard is used for electronics prototyping to make sure your project will work as intended. You'll use it to test out your circuit design by connecting various resistors, ICs, and other devices to it.

You will also need jump wires (or jumper wires) in order to make the connections. Make sure to get them in different colors. Getting used to color coding is an important skill when working with electronics in general.

Safety Rules

The programming component in your projects will be the only truly safe activity. Keep in mind that you will be required to bind parts to each other with a hot soldering iron or hot glue, and you will also have to drill, cut, and work around electricity. No matter how small your project is, you shouldn't take any risks. You can hurt yourself in many ways, and that's why this section on safety rules is necessary. We'll go through all the potentially harmful tasks that you will eventually perform and talk about how to prevent injury.

Working with High Temperatures

Keep in mind that that you will be using your soldering iron a lot, and it heats up to around 450°F (~230°C). Always be aware of it and where you place it. You can burn yourself or damage any other objects lying around. The bigger danger, however, is the solder itself. It's a common mistake to immediately touch around the area you soldered and forget that even the circuit board will heat up around the joint. Wait a couple of minutes after soldering, or you can get some nasty burns.

Another hot material you will work with is the hot glue, and it can be even worse than solder. Always let the glue rest until it hardens. The problem with it is that when you touch it, you don't just experience a burn and then remove your finger. The glue will stick to your skin and burn you until it cools off and solidifies. Always be aware of the placement of your hot tools and the state of your hot binding materials.

Using Sharp Objects

You might be thinking that you cut things on a daily basis, so what could be so different when working with electronics? The thing is that highly sharp precision tools can cause serious injuries, so don't underestimate them. Even an X-ACTO knife can land you at the hospital for stitches.

Always make sure to aim the cutting tool away from yourself and to maintain their sharp edge. It might sound a bit strange, but a dull knife is actually more dangerous than a sharp one. A dull blade tends to slip a lot, and when it does there's a high chance of injuring yourself. A sharpened edge will only sink deeper into whatever you're cutting.

Safety Glasses

Whenever you are working with tools, wear safety glasses. A flying metal fragment from a wire snip is all that's needed to damage your eyesight. Get your hands on a comfortable pair of glasses, or goggles if you prefer them, because you will be wearing them for extended periods of time. They need to protect your precious eyes from injury, but they also need to feel like they aren't there.

Get a Fire Extinguisher

Working with burning hot tools and electricity can be extremely dangerous. All it takes is a spark, or placing your soldering iron on a flammable surface. An even more dangerous item is the battery.

You will be working a lot with batteries, especially with Lithium Polymer ones, and they can be dangerous. All it takes is one mistake that causes a short, and your battery will heat up uncontrollably until it expands. Without a way to cool it immediately, you risk having an explosion on your hands.

So do yourself a favor and get a fire extinguisher as soon as possible, learn how to use one, and check on it regularly to make sure it's functional. Hopefully you will never need it, but it's better to have one handy than to burn your house down or worse.

Ventilate the Area

You will be soldering a lot, and this activity produces a lot of fumes. Solder also contains a bit of lead, and you really don't want to breathe that in on a regular basis. It can't really harm you if you ventilate your workshop, but keep in mind that the fumes are indeed toxic and can cause headaches at the very least. You might also be doing some sanding, painting, drilling and sawing for some of your projects, and breathing in dust is unhealthy.

This doesn't mean you need to buy an expensive, professional ventilation system. Keeping the windows open should suffice. It's important to have a way to let all the smoke and dust particles out instead of breathing them in for hours as you work.

Maintain Order

As you work on more and more Raspberry Pi projects, your workshop will start gathering more and more tools, electronics, tiny components and all sorts of other supplies. Creating a storage method for all of these items is important, not just for the sake of order, but for safety as well. Accidents can easily happen when you have wires and parts lying around everywhere.

Because of all the miniature parts, you should probably start by creating a storage system made out of many small boxes and drawers. You can then keep all your batteries, wires, resistors and so on in their own separate compartment. You should also invest in a label maker and label each container.

Cleanliness is another important aspect of maintaining your working area. You do not want to trip on a power cord when holding a knife or a soldering iron. Establish an area for storing your tools and larger electronics, and always clean up after the day is over.

Practice Soldering

If you've never done any soldering before, you should start practicing as soon as possible, because it takes a bit of time to get good at it. Your first soldering joints might be ugly lumps of solder, but if you dedicate yourself to this "art," you'll improve in no time.

The technique of soldering involves four major steps: surface preparation, surface tinning, connecting the components, and heating the components. Let's discuss each part in more detail:

1. **Surface preparation**: If you are working with wires, they should be stripped from the insulation for about half an inch, or a little over a centimeter. Once you expose the metal wire strands, you should twirl them until they group

together neatly. If you are working with any other metal parts, they should be cleaned first. To guarantee proper soldering and a good connection between parts, you should smooth the metal surface with some fine sandpaper. This will clear any of the roughness, and get rid of any oxidation and other contaminants.

2. **Surface tinning**: This step is about melting a bit of solder onto a surface before you bind it to another surface. You should tin wires especially to ensure a better connection. In order to tin the wire, you should place your hot soldering iron to the bottom part of the wire and hold the solder at the top. The wire will heat up immediately and the solder will cover it.

3. **Connecting the components**: Before soldering, it's always a good idea to first connect parts, such as wires, together mechanically. For instance, you can twist two wires together.

4. **Heating the components**: Always make sure your soldering iron is clean before use. With a clean tip, you can heat up a joint much more efficiently and then place solder on top of it. The heat of the component will melt the solder onto it.

As a bonus step, you should always keep the tip of the iron clean from solder remnants and other impurities that can build up. When the iron is clean, it will be far more efficient at transferring heat to the components.

You do not want to heat up the solder itself, because that can lead to cold joints that eventually fail. A cold joint is when you melt the solder directly and then use the tip of the iron to brush it all over the connection. This is a common beginner mistake, so you should always heat up the part that needs connecting.

Chapter 7

Projects

❀ I ❀ I ❀ I ❀ I ❀ I ❀ I ❀ I ❀ I ❀ I ❀ I ❀ I ❀ I ❀ I ❀ I ❀

Congratulations on learning so much about working with the Raspberry Pi and gaining some programming knowledge with Python! You were also introduced to basic electricity concepts, soldering, and tips on how to maintain a safe working environment so you're ready to make the next step.

In this chapter we will go through several projects that require all the knowledge you gained so far. It's important to put everything you know to the test as soon as you've gathered enough information, because let's face it, humans learn better by doing and not just reading. So let's dive in with your very first project!

Creating a Bot

We discussed electronics and soldering, but your very first project will be something that doesn't require tools - namely, a bot. So what exactly is a bot and what is it used for?

The Internet is an enormous library of information. Everything that has been digitized so far exists somewhere online, but it's not always easy to find. There are billions of web pages, and humans are just not capable of going through all of them. That is why we use computers to do the work for us. Performing repetitive tasks such as crawling web pages, following links, and downloading information is what a bot is for. Do you want to know all the works of a certain author ever published, but don't have the time to do the research? A bot can have a list ready for you while you sleep.

Knowing how to program a bot is a great skill to have, and Python is an amazing language for writing one. We will start by importing the modules you need and get your Raspberry Pi in shape for running a bot to do your bidding.

General Rules

There's a certain etiquette that comes with creating web crawling bots. One of these is that the robots.txt file should be respected. This file is part of most websites and the purpose of it is to allow the owner to restrict bots from visiting certain pages. You want your bot to be accepted by as many websites as possible in order to acquire the information you need. Therefore, you should follow this rule. Otherwise you can be banned from certain websites.

Another rule involves controlling the speed at which your bot requests information. Computers operate really fast, and web servers are sometimes configured poorly without thinking about a fast flow of information. It's considered good practice to limit your bot's speed to requesting around 10 pages per second. This won't be enough to bring down a website.

Lastly, avoid faking your user-agent identity. This is used to identify a website's visitors. Each browser has its own user-agent identity, and bots have their own as well. A lot of websites hide themselves from bots, but by faking this identity you can go through the private pages. You might not suffer any consequences for doing this, but you should be a good citizen of the Internet and not invade anyone's privacy.

The Concept

You should put the concept behind the bot on paper and structure whole logical process before you start programming. Knowing the steps you need to take is half the project and can help you work far more efficiently by knowing which task to focus on.

So how will your bot perform its task? We need to start with a certain webpage, and then determine what kind of file to look for. You can program the file choice, whether it's a .pdf or .mp3, into the bot. The bot will then begin analyzing the page from the start and look for the file format you want. When the file is encountered, the bot is given an instruction to download it to a local directory. This is how the bot will operate while you take a nap or spend time on another activity.

Parsing

This is the process a web bot goes through when reading web pages. A web page is a data stream that your bot needs to know how to read and understand. Writing a simple parsing program is needed in order to parse pages and retrieve relevant links with the information you want. The first thing you need to do to set up a parsing program with Python is to import a library called "Beautiful Soup". Install it by typing the following into your Pi's terminal:

```
sudo apt-get install python-bs4
```

Now you can open your Python editor and import it by typing:

```
import BeautifulSoup
```

If you get an error by any chance, it probably means that you installed a version of the library that is still in its beta release. If this happens type this instead:

```
from bs4 import BeautifulSoup
```

Next up, you need to load a file called doc, which will take the online stream of data and turn it into lines of readable information which can be parsed by the library. Type:

```
import re
doc = [ '<html><head><title> Page Title </title></head>',
    '<body> <p id = "firstpara" align = "center"> This is
paragraph<b>one</b>.',
    '<p id = "secondpara" align = "blah"> This is
paragraph<b>two</b>.',
    </html>']
Soup = BeautifulSoup(".join(doc)) #This is not a double
quote. Use two apostrophes.
print soup.prettify()
```

This last print command is what will redo the webpage to be easy to read, and this is why we need to use the "Beautiful Soup" module.

The "re" module we import at the beginning of this block of code is used for evaluating regular expressions in text. This is probably the best way to search through text-based information and find the relevant strings.

Before You Start Coding

Many web bots exist out there, and you can find examples of them easily. However, in order to learn, you should focus on creating your own from scratch. It might seem a bit challenging at first, because for your bot to work properly, it needs to be able to perform a set of different tasks.

Before you program your bot, you need to decide what files you want your little web crawler to download. You should probably start with free books that are in the public domain. Think of all the text formats you could find your favorite authors' work in. Most files in this case will be .pdf, .txt, .doc, .mobi and .epub. These formats will cover most digital version of the books, whether they are plain text files or Kindle files.

Next up, you should decide where you'll start performing your search for these files. You may be inclined to just say Google, but that is way too broad an area and can add many hours to your bot's hard work. Try to find some kind of web repository or archive that contains all or most of that author's work.

One final thing to consider is where you will store all the information your bot will download. How big is your Raspberry Pi's SD card? If it's only a 4GB card, your storage capabilities might be limited because most of that space will be used to run the operating system. This is why you should invest into a 32GB SD card instead so you don't have any future storage problems. However, even if you have a limited card, you can still connect a flash drive to your Pi. In order to save your bot's downloaded information to an external flash drive, you should just place the bot's script inside any directory found on the drive.

Write Your Bot in Python

We'll start by first importing all the necessary modules that we'll need for the program. Then we will use Python's input command to initiate a browser. Let's see how this looks in code:

```
from bs4 import BeautifulSoup
import time
import mechanize
import urllib
import string
start = http:// + input ("Where should I search?\n")
br = mechanize.Browser()
r = br.open(start)
html = r.read()
```

Now we have the browser object which we called "br" and we can use it to perform various tasks. For instance, we can open a requested page with the br.open instruction. Then we'll read and extract all the data by using the BeautifulSoup module. To achieve this type:

```
soup = BeautifulSoup(html)
for link in soup.find_all("a"):
    print (link.get("href"))
```

You can save what you have so far and try it out to see if it works. Open the terminal and run your bot script. When the program starts, you will be asked to type where to start the search. Type the address of a website like "test.com" and the bot should extract and return you the link.

The next step is to tell the bot to look for actual files and download them. Go back to the previously written code, and right under the "start" line type:

```
filetype = input ("What file type are you looking for?\n")
```

This will ask the user what file type to look for. We already established that .pdf is one of the file formats we want to focus on. So let's return to our code and replace the "for" block with:

```
for link in soup.find_all("a"):
    linkText = str(link)
    if filetype in linkText:
        #download file code
```

The str(link) part of the code is added because we need to convert each link which the Beautiful Soup modules brings to the bot as a link object. This link object needs to be converted to a string in order to be useful. Once we have the link as a string, we can use Python to look through it and find the file type we're looking for.

Next, you'll want to be able to create a list to add more links to it when the bot finds them. Go to your code, and right after the module imports, type the following in order to create a list:

```
linkList = []
if filetype in filename:
    image = rullib.URLopener()
    linkGet = "insert your test link here" + filename
    filesave = string.lstrip(filename, "/")
    image.retrieve (linkGet, filesave)
elif "htm" in filename:
    linkList.append(link)
```

Let's explain this code in more detail. After creating the list we need to add to it, and we do that through "elif" block. If the "filename" will have the type of link you want, the bot will retrieve it. If there isn't one, but there's an "htm" within it, the bot will add it to the "linkList" so that it opens each page and repeats the process. We also use "htm" in our code because it covers .htm as well as .html files. So what do we need next? A function that tells our bot to download files. We already established a download process, however, we are going to repeat it. And what's one of the golden rules we mentioned earlier regarding programming? Never repeat yourself. This is when a function comes in handy. After the linkList, type:

```
def downloadFiles (html, base, filetype, filelist):
    soup = BeautifulSoup (html)
    for link in soup.find_all("a"):
            linkText = str (link.get("href"))
            if filetype in linkText:
                    image = urllib.URLopener()
                    linkGet = base + linkText
                    filesave = string.lstrip (linkText, "/")
                    image.retrieve (linkGet, filesave)
            elif "htm" in linkText
                    linkList.append (link)
```

We're almost done with creating this little web crawler. Next up, you need to parse the linkText in order to get the name of the directory you need. For this process, you can use the os module, which is a library used for manipulating files. Add this to your code:

```
import os
os.makedirs(). #this is used to create a directory
```

You need to have a local directory that is a perfect match with the web directory where the files you are looking for are stored. The directory you need is usually at the beginning of a linkText. For instance, if we have the link /pictures/testing1.html, the directory name is "pictures". So let's instruct the bot to look for slashes:

```
slashList = [ i for I, ind in enumerate(linkText) if ind == "/"]
directoryName = linkText [(slashList[0] + 1) : slashlist[1]]
```

This part of the code basically cuts our previous link example "/pictures/testing1.html" down to just pictures. Now all we need to do is check where we already have a directory that matches the directoryName as in the code. If we don't have one, we tell the bot to create it for us. Type the following right after "directoryName":

```
if not os.path.exists(directoryName):
    os.makedirs(directoryName)
```

The bot is now ready to get to work! Direct it at a website and tell it what files you want. It will start looking for the information you need, create the right the directories for you, and download it all without your help.

Building a Weather Station

Welcome to your first project that requires tools and various electronics. Creating a weather station with the Raspberry Pi is a popular project for beginners. It's fairly easy to build and it puts all the knowledge you acquired to the test. You will have to perform more challenging tasks than simply programming.

Through this project, you will learn how to build a device that can inform you of the wind speed, temperature, barometric pressure and more. The Pi is a great computer for building a weather station because it doesn't demand that much processing power, and it's extremely user-friendly when it comes to connecting all the sensors you'll need.

So what do you need to start making your very own weather station? Well, you have two options. This kind of project is so popular in the Raspberry Pi community that you can already find weather station kits ready for purchase. In this section, however, we're going to take the second path and acquire each part independently. Learning how to work from scratch is a fundamental skill, and kits sometimes make the job a little too easy. It might be more convenient, but your goal is to learn, and you learn by doing. So let's see what the weather station recipe looks like and see what parts you'll need to cook one up.

List of Components

The blueprint for a weather station is fairly simple, and you don't require as many components as other, more complex projects do. However, keep in mind that some of these parts can be a bit expensive. With that being said, let's see what you need.

1. A Raspberry Pi computer with a power adaptor.

2. A magnetometer or a digital compass to be more precise. This is a magnetic sensor, which means it is used to measure magnetism. It can be used to measure the Earth's magnetic field, detect metals with magnetic properties, or as a compass. For this project, you should look for a digital one.

3. A barometric pressure sensor. This device is used to measure the air pressure and it's an important component of any decent weather station.

4. A digital thermometer so that we can measure the temperature, as well as humidity.

5. An optical shaft encoder. This component will be used to measure wind speed.

6. A small breadboard to test the prototype.

7. A square shaft from any hardware store.

8. A pinwheel or any device that can work as a fan.

9. A Lazy Susan bearing.

10. A thin wooden plate.

11. A roughly 12-inch (~30cm) long PVC pipe with a cap. It can be anywhere between 1 to 2 inches (~2.5 - 5 cm) in diameter.

12. Various wires, screws and glues.

Configuring the Pi's I2C Protocol

The I2C is a serial protocol that will allow a multitude of devices to communicate with each other by using only one circuit with a data line, a clock line, and a ground wire. Every connected device is referred to as a node, and normally there's a master node and several slaves. Every slave has its own address, and when the master communicates with one, it needs to first transmit a start line and an address over the data line. The slave responds to the transmission while the rest of the slaves ignore it and wait.

The components that will communicate through this protocol are the barometer and magnetometer. However, you can't simply just plug them in yet. You need to configure your Raspberry Pi so that the protocol works. Type:

```
sudo nano /etc/modules
i2c-bcm2708
i2c-dev
```

Save the file and restart the Pi by using the "sudo shutdown -r now" command. Next, we need to make it possible for the computer to see the devices we're connecting. There's a tool for that and in order to install it, you need open the terminal and type the following instructions:

```
sudo apt-get install python-smbus
sudo apt-get install i2c-tools
```

Now you should be able to start the I2C tool, which is called i2cdetect, and see which devices are connected. If you didn't connect anything yet, you should see a blank list.

The Anemometer

This is a crucial component of your weather station project, because it is used to measure wind speeds. Knowing the speed of the wind can help you determine the real feel of the temperature, and it can also help you calculate how quickly the weather will change. You're not going to build a sophisticated wind speed measuring device. You will only use a rotary shaft encoder, a rotating shaft, and any kind of fins you can find.

How does this rotary shaft encoder work? This part has slits all around a disk's circumference, and when light shines through them, it lands on a receptor found on the opposite side. You can then calculate how fast the disc is spinning by how often the light punches through the slits. Once you connect the fins to the rotating shaft, you need to figure out some wind speeds, because you later need to include them in your program. The easiest way to do this is to have someone drive you around while you measure the speed. You will only need measurements of around 5 to 20 miles per hour.

Let's assemble all of these parts first. You'll need a square shaft that fits perfectly in the square hole of your encoder. Measure the whole and buy the appropriate size from any local hardware store. Afterwards, you need a pinwheel or some kind of windmill that you can attach to the shaft. Check out local hobby or craft stores for this part. Next you'll need a Lazy Susan bearing to make everything rotate. Use a PVC pipe and cut two slots at the end of it so that your encoder can fit tightly, and cap the other end of the pipe. As you can see, you need to have some basic workshop skills for this project, and many others. If you feel a bit confused or clumsy, don't worry, you'll get the hang of it with some practice.

The next step is to connect your anemometer to your Raspberry Pi in order to measure some speeds. You have three wires that need to be connected. The red one from the rotary encoder needs to be connected to the Pi's power pin, the black one goes to the GND, and the white one goes to any GPIO pin you want. We already discussed that the encoder works by sending a signal whenever the light shines through a slit. An encoder of this type usually has 90 slits. Yours might be slightly different, though. In our example with 90 slits, that's also the number of signals you get within one full rotation. Therefore, the number of signals is equal to the number of slits. You will need to take this into account when you write the code that reads the encoder. You need to establish the rotation speed over time, which is measured in seconds. Let's see how that looks in Python code:

```python
import time
import RPI.GPIO as GPIO
GPIO.setmote(GPIO.BOARD)
GPIO.setup(8, GPIO.IN, pull_up_down = GPIO.PUD_DOWN)
prev_input = 0
total = 0
current = time.time()
while True:
    input = GPIO.input(8)
    if ((not prev_input) and input):
            print ("turning")
            total = total + 1
    prev_input = input
    if total == 90:
    print (1/(time.time() - current)), "revolutions per sec"
            total = 0
            current = time.time()
```

The most important part in this code is the while loop, so let's discuss it in more detail. We first set the prev_input to 0, which means that the disc isn't moving. When it's set to 1, it means that it is rotating. When that happens, we have to increment the total, set the prev_input to input, and continue the while loop after checking whether we reached 90 signals yet. If an entire round of 90 signals occurred, then we have one single revolution, which allows us to do the math and print the revolutions per second. Afterwards, we reset the total and current. You can test this code by running the script after you connect the device to your Raspberry Pi. Give the rotary encoder a spin while the script is being executed, and you should see results.

If everything is working as intended so far, it's time to correlate the revolutions per second with wind speed. The simplest way to achieve that, as mentioned before, is to get a friend to drive you around. Run the script and hold the device outside the car window while driving at 5 MPH for a few minutes. Do this again at 10, 15 and 20 MPH. For instance, at 5 MPH, you should get around 5.8 revolutions per second.

Now how do you get the wind speed out of all this? Let's just say it involves using an inverse logarithmic function. The purpose of this project isn't to bore you with math, so here's the formula you'll be using within the final code: wind speed $= e^{((y+0.95)/4.3)}$. We'll get back to this later.

The Digital Compass

In this project, we're going to use a compass to determine the direction of the wind. You should look over the I2C protocol section for this, because we're going to use it again for the compass.

Now let's start with a bit of soldering. Solder the male headers of the compass to the HMC breakout board. Afterwards, you can make the connection between the pins and the Pi by using jumper wires. Connect the VCC (voltage at the common collector) line to the Pi's #2 pin, and the GND (ground) line to the #6 pin. Then connect the SDA (data) line to the #3 pin, and the SCL (clock) line to the #5 pin. Now that all the necessary connections have been established, you can use the smbus module in Python to read the compass with the help of some math.

The next step is to make a separate directory where you will keep all the data coming from your weather station. We discussed earlier in the book how to make a directory, but here's an example in case you need a refresher:

```
cd ~
mkdir weather
cd weather
```

Now go to this new directory and create a Python script inside it, and let's write the code for the weather station.

```python
import smbus
import math
bus = smbus.SMBus(0)
address = 0x1e
def read_byte(adr):
    return bus.read_byte_data (address, adr)
def read_word(adr):
    high = bus.read_byte_data (address, adr)
    low = bus.read_byte_data (address, adr + 1)
    val = (high << 8) + low
    return val
def read_word_2c(adr):
    val = read_word(adr)
if (val >= 0x8000):
return -((65535 - val) + 1)
else:      return val
def write_byte(adr, value):
bus.write_byte_data(address, adr, value)
write_byte (0, 0b01110000)
write_byte (1, 0b00100000)
write_byte (2, 0b00000000)
scale = 0.92
x_offset = -39
y_offset = -100
x_out = (read_word_2c(3) - x_offset) * scale
y_out = (read_word_2c(7) - y_offset) * scale
bearing = math.atan2(y_out, x_out)
if bearing < 0:
bearing += 2 * math.pi
```

```
print "Bearing: ", math.degrees(bearing)
```

This block of code may seem a bit confusing, so let's try to break it down a little and understand the concept behind it. First, we import the "smbus" and "math" modules, because we need them to read from and write to the sensor's address. All the read functions we created are used to read and write byte (8-bit) values to the sensor's address. The write functions are then used to write the very specific values of 112, 32 and 0 with the purpose to configure the sensor for reading. The values we used aren't random, they come listed with the I2C sensor. Next up we get the compass readings (on the x and y axis) and calculate the sensor's bearing with an inverse tangent (atan2).

Run the program with a compass near you so you can see whether the readings are accurate. You can point the board with the side that has the soldered headers. Depending on the readings, you might have to adjust the x_offset and y_offset in order to adjust the bearing correctly. Now your weather station can figure out the wind's direction! Mount the compass on top of the anemometer's rotating shaft, and you will be able to get the proper readings.

The Temperature and Humidity Sensor

For this part of the project, we will no longer use the I2C protocol, but you will have to solder the headers in the same manner as you did with the digital compass. Once you're done, you have to connect the sensor's VCC pin to the Raspberry Pi's #2 pin, the

GND pin to the Pi's #6 pin, CLK pin to the Pi's #7 pin, and DATA pin to the Pi's #11 pin.

The next step is to install the rpiSht1x Python module inside your weather station directory. Now let's discuss the code for measuring the temperature and humidity with a digital thermometer:

```
from sht1x.Sht1x import Sht1x as SHT1x
dataPin = 11
clkPin = 7
sht1x = SHT1x(dataPin, clkPin, SHT1x.GPIO_BOARD)
temperature = sht1x.read_temperature_C()
humidity = sht1x.read_humidity()
dewPoint = sht1x.calculate_dew_point(temperature,
humidity)
temperature = temperature * 9 / 5 + 32    #use this if you
want your temp in degrees F
print ("Temperature: {} Humidity: {} Dew Point:
{}".format(temperature, humidity, dewPoint)
```

Save this block of code as sht.py and run it with the "sudo python sht.py" instruction. Here we use the functions read_temperature_C(), read_humidity(), and calculate_dew_point() to gain values from the sensor. Afterwards, the program converts the values and displays the results.

Setting Up the Barometer

Probably the best way to observer changes in weather is by measuring and analyzing the air pressure. For instance, if it drops, a storm might be coming, and if it increases, good weather is heading towards you. The barometer chip uses the I2C protocol, so you'll have to wire it in the following manner. Once you soldered the headers, connect the VCC pin to the Pi's #1 pin, the GND pin to the Pi's #6 pin, the SDA to pin #3, and the SCL to pin #5.

Next up, you have to download and install some Python libraries. In our example we'll use a common barometer chip BMP180, which works with the BMP085 module. Once you've installed it, create a new Python script in your weather station directory and type the following code:

```
from Adafruit_BMP085 import BMP085
bmp = BMP085(0x77)
temp = bmp.readTemperature()
temp = temp*9/5 + 32      #if you're not in one of the 99% of
countries using Celsius pressure = bmp.readPressure()
altitude = bmp.readAltitude()
print "Temperature:            %.2f F" % temp
print "Pressure:     %.2f hPa" %(pressure / 100.0)
print "Altitude:     %.2f" %altitude
```

This code works pretty much in the same manner as the script for the thermometer. We use an imported library and its functions to read the values we need from the barometer.

Put Everything Together

Connecting everything together on a rotating platform is important, especially when you want to adequately measure the speed of the wind. The best way to assemble all the pieces together is to use a breadboard. Connect all your chips to it and then connect the board to your Pi. This way you can easily mount the entire ensemble of electronics on a platform. All you have left to do now is run and take out your weather station for a spin, and make it your goal to put meteorologists to shame.

Creating a Security System

In today's modern age, it's almost necessary to turn your house into a smart home with top security features. Installing video cameras that are streaming to a laptop or a phone is commonplace, and we rely on all kinds of sensors for our safety.

Motion detectors, trip alarms, and information gathering sensors such as those that measure air quality and warn you about carbon monoxide leaks are only a few other examples of home security systems. Having a safe living space improved by technology can lift some of the stress off your shoulders.

The Raspberry Pi just happens to be an ideal tool for creating a security system. Test your knowledge of what you learned so far and practice your skills without digging too deep into your wallet. Home security can be extremely expensive, but with this project you will see that it really doesn't take all that much to create a good system.

This kind of project, just like the weather station in the previous section, relies on the concept of a sensor network. As you've already seen, the Pi is a great computer for interfacing many sensors that fulfill specific tasks. Your home desktop and/or laptop has been left without the modules needed to make the required connections. However, with the Pi, all you need is a motion sensor that connects to its GPIO pins, and with a few lines of clever Python code, you improve the security of your home.

Because processing power isn't so important for this project, we will include in our security system an infrared motion sensor, a magnetic sensor, a limit switch and a pressure switch. The motion detecting sensor will be placed anywhere on the ground. The pressure sensor can be used in the doorway where an unwelcome "guest" will step when entering your home. The magnetic sensor is great at detecting when a window or a door opens. And finally, the limit switch can determine if a trip wire is touched. On top of using a bunch of sensors, we will set up a text messaging system through which the Pi will notify you when something happens to the security system.

List of Components

Here's what you'll need for this home security system, other than your Raspberry Pi:

1. A Raspberry Pi camera module.

2. A magnetic sensor.

3. A motion sensor.

4. A pressure switch.

5. A limit switch.

6. An Ethernet cable, possibly a long one.

7. Jumper wires and various connectors.

Some of these are optional. You can ignore some sensors and switches if you don't want to include them, or you can even expand your security system to add more of them. It's your call, because this is a highly customizable project.

Wireless Network Connection

Any good home security system needs to be connected to a wireless network. Your Pi will control the system and will send you notifications when any sensor is triggered. You can establish either a direct cable network connection, or a wireless one. In this day and age you might want to go with the wireless network. Let's just say that you don't want an intruder to be able to just cut your Ethernet cable and make your entire security system pointless.

First, you will need a USB wireless dongle. It's an inexpensive device and you won't have any trouble configuring it. The next thing you want for this network, is to set your Pi to a static IP address. Why? Because this way you'll be able to log in to your computer remotely no matter what. If you stick to a dynamic IP, it might change if your Pi is rebooted and then you won't know the new address when you want to log in. So let's start by configuring your static IP address. Type:

```
sudo nano /etc/network/interfaces
iface wlano inet dhcp #change this to following line
iface wlano inet static
address 190.162.2.60 (use any address you want, this is just
an example)
netmask 255.255.255.0 (your netmask if it's different)
network 190.162.2.60 (this is your network location)
broadcast 190.162.2.255 (you can find out your broadcast
value by typing ifconfig)
gateway 190.162.2.1 (use the IP address of your router)
```

Save these files and restart your Pi. Check with the ifconfig command to see if all the changes have been made. Don't forget to write down your static IP!

The next step is to have an SSH server running in order to use the static IP. Open the terminal and type:

```
sudo raspi-config
```

This will start up the configuration tool. Head to advanced options, then to #4 SSH and make sure this is enabled. Finish the configuration and restart your Pi with a "sudo reboot" command. Your SSH server should now be operational. You can connect to your Pi remotely using a Windows or Mac machine. We already discussed this in an earlier chapter in this book.

Connect the Motion Sensor

Motion detection is probably one of the most important features of a good security system. However, keep in mind that you can't rely on a motion sensor alone. You don't want a little bird or a cat to make you panic because you don't have any other system to verify what happened.

So how does a motion sensor actually work? Basically, it detects changes in the infrared levels emitted by the objects within the area. A signal is sent whenever a change is detected. Most of these sensors have three pins, namely a VCC (+), GND (-) and Output (OUT). You first want to connect the GND to the Pi's #6 pin, which you might already know is the ground pin. Then connect the VCC pin to the Pi's #2 pin and the OUT pin to any GPIO pin. Let's create a basic test to see how the motion sensor will work. All you need is an LED connected to a breadboard and a bit of code to tell the LED to light up when motion is detected. Create a new python script and type the following code:

```
import RPi.GPIO as GPIO
import time
GPIO.setwarnings (False) #eliminates some complaints from
the library
GPIO.setmode (GPIO.BOARD)
GPIO.setup (11, GPIO.IN, pull_up_down=GPIO.PUD_UP)
GPIO.setup (13, GPIO.OUT)
while True:
if GPIO.input (11):
GPIO.output (13, 1)
else:
GPIO.output (13, 0)
```

For the test, you will want to connect the + pin of the sensor to the Pi's #2 pin, then the OUT pin to the #11 pin. The - pin has to be connected to any ground line on the breadboard. Then connect the Pi's #13 pin to the positive arm of the LED, through a resistor, and the negative arm to a ground line. Now open the terminal and run your script with the "sudo" command. To jog your memory, we need the "sudo" command because you need to access the GPIO pins. If all is working as it should, the LED should now light up when you pass your hand in front of the motion sensor and then turn off after a while when there's no more movement.

We can now leave this part of the project as it is and move on to the limit switch.

The Limit Switch

What is this device for, exactly? Well, you might be using one a lot because a lot of cool Pi projects that involve robots will require a limit switch. It is normally used to detect the limit of movement. So if we take a robot as an example, it needs to know when it's close to a certain object or when it's about to crash into the wall. It works in a fairly simple way. The switch's default state is open, letting no power through, and it has a lever that protrudes from the body of the device. When this lever is pressed, it is closed and voltage is sent through the circuit. In our project, this voltage will be sent to the Pi's input pin. In other words, the lever will allow objects that are a set distance away to close the contact of the switch.

In this project, however, we're not going to use the switch to see when something gets too close to it. We're going to check whether a trip wire has been pulled because, after all, we're trying to build a home security system. This part of the project might take you back to some memories of watching the "Home Alone" movies, so enjoy it.

Mount the switch to the wall, somewhere where you can extend a wire of fishing line to the opposite part of the wall. The best places for a trip wire are entrances or windows. You need to attach the line to the lever of the switch. Then you need to position the switch in such a way that the lever is pulled down to activate the switch when the wire is tripped.

Keep in mind that this device is not a sensor, but a physical switch. They are made out of really basic components, such as metal springs that bounce a few times before they make a steady contact. What does this mean for us? That there are some interruptions when the contact is being made, meaning the switch goes back and forth from on to off several times before settling. We need to take this into account when writing the code. This process is called "debouncing" and we need to write a script that knows to read the signal only when the switch is no longer bouncing. Here's how the code would look:

```
import time
prev_input = 0 while True:
#take a reading
input = GPIO.input(11)
#if the last reading was low and this one is high, print
if ((not prev_input) and input):
print("Button pressed")
#update the previous input
prev_input = input
#allow time to debounce
time.sleep(0.05)
```

This small block of code is all about ignoring the button press if it happens in less than 0.05 seconds before the previous one. Let's now get the switch working by connecting it to the right GPIO pins and writing some more code. Connect the Pi's #2 pin to the left pin of the switch, and then connect the switch's middle pin to the Pi's #11 pin. We can ignore the right pin of the switch, as it's not

```
import time
import RPi.GPIO as GPIO
GPIO.setwarnings (False)
GPIO.setmode (GPIO.BOARD)
GPIO.setup (11, GPIO.IN, pull_up_down =
GPIO.PUD_DOWN)
prev_input = 0
while True:
input = GPIO.input (11)
if ((not prev_input) and input):
print "Button pressed"
    prev_input = input
time.sleep (0.05)
```

When you press the switch's lever, your program should now print "Button pressed". Now we can set up the pressure switch.

The Pressure Switch

This switch works almost like the limit switch, however, they look quite different. The pressure switch we'll be using looks like a square pad, and it registers pressure changes as changes in voltage. To connect it, just link one of the switch's leads to the Pi's #2 pin and the other lead to the #11 pin.

Now how will our code look for the pressure switch? Exactly the same! That's right, you don't have to write separate code for this device. Just plug it in, run the script you wrote for the limit switch, and press on the pad. You should now detect a change in pressure. You can then place the pad wherever you want. Most people set it under the entrance mat.

The Magnetic Sensor

This device alerts you when it detects a change in the magnetic field within an area. In our case, it can be used to detect when two metal pieces move away from each other. So let's say we set it up for the window. When it opens, the sensor will detect the change and alert you. Keep in mind that these sensors usually come with two small magnets that will be used to prevent false readings.

Start by connecting the sensor's wires to the Pi. The red wire goes to the #2 pin, black to #6 and white to pin #11. Again, we can reuse code. This is the beauty of programming. You don't always have to write everything from scratch. Code can be reusable, even if you have to just make some slight modifications. In this case, we're going to take the script for the switch and make the following changes:

```
import time
import RPi.GPIO as GPIO
GPIO.setwarnings (False)
GPIO.setmode (GPIO.BOARD)
GPIO.setup (11, GPIO.IN, pull_up_down =
GPIO.PUD_DOWN)
prev_input = 0
while True:
```

```
input = GPIO.input (11)
if ((not prev_input) and input):
print "Field changed"
    prev_input = input
time.sleep (0.05)
```

Run the script and experiment by running a magnet in front of the sensors. It might take a while to figure out which distance is just right to fit your purpose. Once you know the correct distance, you will be know where to mount the magnet.

Camera Setup

You can use the Pi to work with a small camera and take pictures or video footage. You'll need to find a good place to position the Pi, but luckily it's such a small computer that you shouldn't really have any trouble figuring out a location. For this setup to work, you will need the wireless function that you learned how to set up earlier as well as the camera.

You can use the "raspi-config" tool to configure the camera. After you enable it, you'll have two commands to work with. One is for capturing pictures, and the other is used to capture video footage. For the sake of this project, we will take only pictures, because streaming video would require additional software and more complex configurations. Here's how simple the script is for taking still frames:

```
from subprocess import call
call (["raspistill -o image.jpg"], shell = True)
```

"Raspistill" is a command you can try even from the terminal, but we need a script so that we can tell the Pi to take pictures automatically. The image that is taken will be called "image.jpg" and will be stored in the same directory as the script. You can then call this script whenever any of the sensors is tripped, and the camera will take a picture.

Receiving Messages

This part of the project is probably the most interesting, because we're going to tell the Pi to send out a text message when something happens to the security network. Receiving a notification will warn you that something happened, and then you can determine whether it was just a bird, or you need to call the police because someone is breaking in.

The concept behind our messaging system is simple. We tell the Pi to use the local network to send out an email, which will then be translated into a text message by your mobile service. You need two things to set this up: an email account (Gmail for instance), and the knowledge of how to send an SMS through email with your mobile carrier. In most cases, you need to send an email to a carrier's specific address in order to have it delivered as a text message. Now let's see how this notification system will look in code. Type:

133

```
def send_text(str):
HOST = "smtp.gmail.com"
SUBJECT = "Break-in!"
TO = "xxxxxxxxxx@txt.att.net"
FROM = "email@example.com"
text = str
BODY = string.join(("From: %s" % FROM, "To: %s" % TO,
"Subject: %s" % SUBJECT, "", text), "\r\n")
s = smtplib.SMTP("smtp.gmail.com",587)
s.set_debuglevel(1)
s.ehlo()
s.starttls()
s.login("username@gmail.com", "mypassword")
s.sendmail(FROM, [TO], BODY)
s.quit()
```

This code needs to be modified based on the services you are using. In this example, we use a Gmail account with an AT&T mobile carrier. Keep in mind that Gmail's smtp access is through port 587, so if you use a different service, you will also have to make the correct modification.

Piece Everything Together

So far we worked on each individual component. Now we need to combine all the pieces together to have one, complete home security system. For this part of the project, you'll need some Ethernet cable to make all the connections.

Start by stripping the cable of its outer layer. You'll then need to use a breadboard, because we want everything to share the ground. Look for a great spot where you can set up your Pi, especially considering you will want to plug it in because batteries can't last long enough for a security system to be efficient. Also keep in mind that the spot needs to offer the perfect angle for the Pi's camera.

Next, find all the right spots for all the sensors you are going to use. The distance between them and the Pi doesn't matter. You will have to run the Ethernet cable from the Pi to each sensor no matter what. Make sure to connect all the negative wires to the common ground row on your breadboard, and then connect the positive wires to GPIO pins. Writing down a little schematic on how everything is going to be set up will be of great help, because you will need the references when you put all the separate blocks of code together. Once you're done with the connections, here's how your code should look for the entire security assembly:

```
import time
import RPi.GPIO as GPIO
from subprocess import call
import string
import smtplib
GPIO.setwarnings (False)
GPIO.setmode (GPIO.BOARD)
time_stamp = time.time() #used for debouncing
#set pins
#pin 11 = motion sensor
GPIO.setup (11, GPIO.IN, pull_up_down=GPIO.PUD_DOWN)
```

```python
#pin 13 = magnetic sensor
GPIO.setup (13, GPIO.IN, pull_up_down=GPIO.PUD_DOWN)
#pin 15 = limit switch
GPIO.setup (15, GPIO.IN,
pull_up_down=GPIO.PUD_DOWN)
#pin 19 = pressure switch
GPIO.setup (19, GPIO.IN,
pull_up_down=GPIO.PUD_DOWN)
def take_pic(sensor):
call(["raspistill -o image" + sensor + ".jpg"], shell=True)
time.sleep(0.5) #wait 1/2 second for pic to be taken before
continuing
def send_text(details):
HOST = "smtp.gmail.com"
SUBJECT = "Break-in!"
TO = "xxxxxxxxxx@txt.att.net"
FROM = "email@mydomain.com"
text = details
BODY = string.join(("From: %s" % FROM, "To: %s" % TO,
"Subject: %s" % SUBJECT, "", text), "\r\n")
s = smtplib.SMTP("smtp.gmail.com",587)
s.set_debuglevel(1)
s.ehlo()
s.starttls()
s.login("username@gmail.com", "mypassword")
s.sendmail(FROM, [TO], BODY)
s.quit()
def motion_callback(channel):
global time_stamp
time_now = time.time()
```

```python
    if (time_now - time_stamp) >= 0.3: #check for debouncing
        print "Motion detector detected."
        send_text("Motion detector")
        take_pic("motion")
        time_stamp = time_now
def limit_callback(channel):
    global time_stamp
    time_now = time.time()
    if (time_now - time_stamp) >= 0.3: #check for debouncing
        print "Limit switch pressed."
        send_text("Limit switch")
        take_pic("limit")
        time_stamp = time_now
def magnet_callback(channel):
    global time_stamp
    time_now = time.time()
    if (time_now - time_stamp) >= 0.3: #check for debouncing
        print "Magnetic sensor tripped."
        send_text("Magnetic sensor")
        take_pic("magnet")
        time_stamp = time_now
#this is the main body
raw_input("Press enter to start program\n")
GPIO.add_event_detect(11, GPIO.RISING,
callback=motion_callback) GPIO.add_event_detect(13,
GPIO.RISING, callback=magnet_callback)
GPIO.add_event_detect(15, GPIO.RISING,
callback=limit_callback)
# the pressure switch ends the program
```

```
# you could easily add a unique callback for the pressure
switch
# and add another switch just to turn off the network
try:
print "Waiting for sensors..."
GPIO.wait_for_edge(19, GPIO.RISING)
except KeyboardInterrupt:
GPIO.cleanup()
GPIO.cleanup()
```

The Radio-Controlled Airplane

This is probably the coolest of all the projects, because who hasn't ever dreamt of flying? Sadly, flight schools can be very expensive, and not everyone can become a pilot even with the cash on hand. Flying a built to scale radio controlled airplane model will have to be enough instead. However, just flying a model might get boring after a while, and that is why this project will be more than that.

Because of the Pi's camera, we're going to program our plane to do more than just flying. We will tell the plane to take pictures during flight. On top of that, we will also install a GPS receiver onboard in order to track the flight trajectory and later load it into Google Earth.

Keep in mind that for this project, we are going to use the more advanced concepts of object-oriented programming. However, just in case the earlier chapter that explained these concepts wasn't enough, you will still be guided through the code in order to understand it better. Now let's see what we need to build a radio-controlled airplane and get it up in the sky as soon as possible!

Your Shopping List

This project will be a bit more expensive than the others. There won't be so many parts, but you will need an actual radio-controlled plane, which can drain your budget. Nonetheless, you can always build this project over time or learn to improvise with smaller plane or drones. Here's what you'll need:

1. A raspberry Pi with a camera.

2. A GPS receiver with an antenna. The antenna is optional however.

3. A medium size RC plane.

4. An RC battery and a 5V regulator that will be used to power the Pi.

As you can see, the shopping list is a lot shorter than it was for the other projects, however the RC plane can be pricey, unless you already have one of course. If you are going to invest into one, try to find one that is sturdy and can handle a few small crashes. A beginner might have issues handling the plane properly. However, what really matters for this project is having the power needed to carry the extra weight of a Raspberry Pi, GPS receiver, and the battery that is used to power everything.

Another thing to consider is the positioning of the plane's wings. If you have one with a top configuration, you'll have an easier time positioning the Pi and all its attachments on top of the plane.

Now let's start by making a new directory for this project. We'll call it:

```
mkdir plane
```

The GPS Receiver

The receiver needs to be connection to the Pi, but how do we achieve this? We need to use a Python module called "gpsd" and the Pi's universal asynchronous receiver/ transmitter (UART) interface, namely pins 7 and 8. This gpsd module will allow us to access the data that is transmitted by the GPS receiver. As for the interface, it consists of a + and - power connection and pins for transmitting and receiving. Before we configure the interface, we need to download the right software that is needed to read all the components and the programs associated with them. Type in the terminal:

```
sudo apt-get install gpsd gpsd-clients python-gps
```

Now we can configure the UART interface. It already starts getting a bit tricky here, because the interface is set to connect to a terminal window, but we want access to the transmit and receive pins. So to start setting everything up for our purpose, we first need to make a copy of /boot/cmdline.txt. You can do that by typing:

```
sudo cp /boot/cmdline.txt /boot/cmdlinecopy.txt
```

Afterwards, edit it by typing:

```
sudo nano /boot/cmdline.txt
```

And delete this segment:

```
Console=ttyAMAO, 115200 kgdboc = ttyAMAO, 115200
```

The file should read like this:

141

```
dwc_otg.lpm_enable=0 console=tty1 root=/dev/mmcblkop2
rootfstype=ext4 elevator=deadline rootwait
```

Save the file. Next up, edit the inittab file by typing:

```
sudo nano /etc/inittab
```

You will have to comment out the last line of code. This line instructs the computer to start the terminal connection. Just type a # symbol in front of the line and it won't be executed. It should look like this:

```
#T0:23:respawn:/sbin/getty -L ttyAMA0 115200 vt100
```

Now restart the Pi with the usual "sudo shutdown -r now" command line.

The next step is to connect the receiver to the computer. Here are the steps you need to take:

1. The GPS receiver's VIN goes to the Pi's #2 pin.

2. The GND goes to the Pi's #6 pin.

3. The Tx (transmit) goes to the Pi's RX (receive) which is pin #10.

4. The Rx of the receiver then goes to the Pi's Tx, which is pin #8.

You should now have power for the receiver and its LED should start to blink. Next up, you need to run the GPS client. Type:

```
cgps -s
```

This is a simple program that will take the data and display it to you. If you don't get any information and see only zeros, it means that you can't get a satellite fix. Give it a few minutes, or go outside under the clear sky. If you still have signal issues, an antenna will fix the problem.

The next step is to create a way for the GPS to communicate with the Pi and make the information readable to the user. The cgps client we used is only good for testing purposes because it's difficult to get any usable data from it. What we need is a program that can store the data to be later used in Google Earth. So let's set up a log file for this purpose by typing:

```
import logging
logging.basicConfig(filename='locations.log',level=logging.
DEBUG,format='%(message)s')
```

So what do these lines of code actually do? They import the module, declare the file name and the data that will get logged, and then give the format of every line. Every GPS signal will be save in three different strings, which are longitude, latitude, and altitude. These are the 3 coordinates we will need to use with Google Earth later. If you need more information on logging, you can check out Python's library on it through the help system.

Google Earth and KML Files

As we discussed earlier, we want to use Google Earth to analyze our plane's flight record. However, Google Earth can't read our log file yet. We need to format it in a KML file, which is used by Google to delineate landmarks and paths. KML files are similar to XML, and you can recognize them due to their similarity to HTML because they both use <> as tags for information types. Lucky for us, we actually already formatted the file to have only longitude, latitude, and altitude separated by spaces. So let's write each line to a new file that we'll name "kml":

```
kml.write ("<Document> whatever you want
</Document>\n")
```

Next, we want to write the code that will instruct the program to take a picture and log the GPS position every 30 seconds. Because we're recording information at certain intervals of time, we'll use KML's path function to create a visual representation of the route the plane took. We're going to use 30 seconds intervals in order to create a neat trajectory representation, because this way the path connections will be made out of straight lines. For instance, we will clearly see how the plane goes from point A to point B to point C and so on. You should fly your plane over a neat grassy field for the

144

best results, and to reduce the chances of crashing your plane into solid concrete.

Threading and Objects

For this project we will have to use a programming feature called threading. Threads are valuable because they allow your computer processor to perform a multitude of tasks at the same time. Without threads, all the processing power would be tied to one task at a time. All you really need to do is make a call to "import threading" to have access to them.

In this program, we need to take advantage of threads in order to poll the GPS receiver. By using a thread, the main buffer will be able to continuously gather data, and log it into a separate file for later use. Our aim is to create an object that will request data from the receiver every 30 seconds. Let's see how all of this looks in Python:

```
class myObject(threading.Thread):
def __init__(self):
#function used to initiate the class and
threadthreading.Thread.__init__(self) #needed to start the
thread
def run(self): #function performed while thread is running
```

This is our thread object that we will start from the main part of the program by declaring a new thread.

```
newObject = myObject()
newObject.start()
```

This thread will now run with an instance of "myObject" called "newObject". The thread will be initiated with "threading.Thread._init(self). The program will continue to collect GPS data and take pictures until we quit it.

Automatic Startup

For this project, we will need a way to automatically start the GPS logging script, because we won't have a monitor or a keyboard connected to the Pi. To set this up, you will need to make an entry to the /etc/rc.local file. For this example, the GPS logging code is named getGPS.py and is stored in the Documents/plane directory, so we will add the following line:

```
/home/pi/Documents/plane/getGPS.py
```

Next up, open the rc.local file like this:

```
sudo nano /etc/rc.local
```

And add the following line before the last exit line:

```
python /home/pi/Documents/plane/getGPS.py
```

We also need the line which we used earlier to test the generic GPS client at the beginning of this project. Type the following line into /etc/rc.local:

```
sudo gpsd /dev/ttyAMAo -F /var/run/gpsd.sock
```

Now wait for the GPS to get a signal from a satellite. This can take around half a minute, maybe more. We need to take this into account for this step of the project to work as intended. Therefore, your final version of /etc/rc.local file should look like this:

```
sudo gpsd /dev/ttyAMAo - F /var/run/gpsd/sock
sleep 45
python /home/pi/Documents/plane/getGPS.py
```

"Sleep 45" will tell the script to wait for 45 seconds before running. Save the file and exit. Now whenever you start up, the script will work automatically.

Piece Everything Together

If you have your radio-controlled plane, piecing everything together is a fairly simple process. You need a battery connected to the Pi and a regulator to make sure you don't overcharge. Li-Po batteries with 1.3A per hour are perfect for this job. A voltage regulator is something you can get from any electronics store, or improvise with a USB car charger. The central terminal needs to be connected to the battery's positive (+) lead, and one of the outer terminals goes to GND. Then you use a USB cable to make the connection with the Pi, and you will have the juice.

Now you'll have to strap everything to the plane. This will depend entirely on your model and type of plane. Just keep in mind that balance matters, so whatever you do, try not to disrupt the airflow over the wings and distribute the weight over the plane as evenly as you can. For instance, you can place the GPS on the nose of the plane, the Pi on the middle section, and the camera somewhere on the belly of the plane, pointing downwards towards the ground. It might not look pretty, but it does the job.

When you're all set, power up the Pi and wait for 45 seconds for the script to start and for the GPS to connect to a satellite. Then enjoy flying and taking some pictures! When you land and return home, you will be able to run the kml conversion and open the plane's log file, parse the text, and write all the locations down into a .kml file. Then you can use this file on any computer with Google Earth.

Here's the final code for the plane program:

```
import os
from gps import *
from time import *
import time
import threading
import logging from subprocess
import call
#set up logfile
```

```python
logging.basicConfig(filename='locations.log',
level=logging.DEBUG,
format='%(message)s')
picnum = o
gpsd = None
class GpsPoller(threading.Thread):
    def __init__(self): #initializes thread
    threading.Thread.__init__(self)
    global gpsd
    gpsd = gps(mode=WATCH_ENABLE)
    self.current_value = None
    self.running = True
    def run(self): #actions taken by thread
    global gpsd
    while gpsp.running:
    gpsd.next()
if __name__ == '__main__': #if in the main program section,
gpsp = GpsPoller() #start a thread and start logging
try:  #and taking pictures
gpsp.start()
while True:
#log location from GPS
logging.info(str(gpsd.fix.longitude) + " " +
str(gpsd.fix.latitude) + " " + str(gpsd.fix.altitude))
#save numbered image in correct directory
call(["raspistill -o /home/pi/Documents/plane/image" +
str(picnum) + ".jpg"], shell=True)
picnum = picnum + 1  #increment picture number
time.sleep(3)
except (KeyboardInterrupt, SystemExit):
```

```
gpsp.running = False
gpsp.join()
```

Here's the final code for the KML conversion program:

```
import string
#open files for reading and writing
gps = open('locations.log', 'r')
kml = open('plane.kml', 'w')
kml.write('<?xml version="1.o" encoding="UTF-8" ?>\n')
kml.write('<kml
xmlns="http://www.opengis.net/kml/2.2">\n')
kml.write('<Document>\n')
kml.write('<name>Plane Path</name>\n')
kml.write('<description>Path taken by
plane</description>\n')
kml.write('<Style id="yellowLineGreenPoly">\n')
kml.write('<LineStyle<color>7fooffff</color><width>4</widt
h></LineStyle>\n')
kml.write('<PolyStyle><color>7fooffoo</color></PolyStyle>\
n')
kml.write('</Style>\n')
kml.write('Placemark><name>Plane Path</name>\n')
kml.write('<styleUrl>#yellowLineGreenPoly</styleUrl>\n')
kml.write('<LineString>\n')
kml.write('<extrude>1</extrude><tesselate>1</tesselate>\n'
)
kml.write('<altitudeMode>relative</altitudeMode>\n')
kml.write('<coordinates>\n')
```

```python
for line in gps:
#separate string by spaces
coordinate = string.split(line)
longitude = coordinate[0]
latitude = coordinate[1]
altitude = coordinate[2]
kml.write(longitude + "," + latitude + "," + altitude + "\n")
kml.write('<\coordinates>\n')
kml.write('</LineString>\n')
kml.write('</Placemark>\n')
kml.write('</Document>\n')
kml.write('</kml>\n')
```

Conclusion

❖ । ❖ । ❖ । ❖ । ❖ । ❖ । ❖ । ❖ । ❖ । ❖ । ❖ । ❖ । ❖ । ❖ । ❖ । ❖

Congratulations for making it all the way to the end of this book! It couldn't have been easy with so much technical information on various topics, but you deserve to reward yourself for the effort. Hopefully the content was illuminating enough to get you started working with the Raspberry Pi. Don't forget, however, that skipping through the information or just reading it isn't enough. The value of practice cannot be overstated, so continue to work on new programming exercises and build new projects. It can be extremely challenging, but if you take it one step at a time, you can overcome any hurdle.

Transmitting technical information through text can be difficult, especially on the reader's side, so don't rely on this book alone. It should be enough to guide you through the entire process of working with the Raspberry Pi and basic as well as some advanced programming concepts, however the written word sometimes isn't perfect for sharing advanced data. So expand your knowledge by taking advantage of the online wealth of resources on programming with Python. Find groups where you can discuss and collaborate.

Watch videos that can clarify the process of soldering and other techniques much clearer than text.

With all that being said, let's summarize what you already learned with the help of this book:

In the first section of the book, you learned all about the Raspberry Pi, the various models available to you, and how to set one up. This kind of computer may be different from what you're used to, but the first chapters guided you on how to start working with the Pi. You learned important networking concepts and techniques that will help you when you work on projects that require a remote connection. You learned about the Linux operating system, which might be new to you, and you now know how to issue basic commands. It's not quite as popular as Windows or Apple's operating system, therefore it is important for you to feel as comfortable with it as you are with your main computer.

In the second part of the book, we focused on the topic of programming. We started out with the basics of working with Python and explained all the important concepts which you need to understand in order to build a solid foundation. Keep in mind that everything you learned in this section can be applied to any programming language. It is much easier to learn how to program with C++, C# or Java if you already know the basics from Python, for instance. Hopefully you also did some exercises to solidify this newly acquired knowledge. Programming requires practice, and it is not enough to just read the theory and copy the code as you go along. Take extra time to progress at a slower pace, because practice takes time. This becomes even more important when we talk about the advanced concepts behind object oriented programming. In this book, we didn't go into too much detail, because for the purpose of learning how to work with the Raspberry Pi, it's mostly enough to know the basics. Keep in mind however, that if you plan to develop your programming skills and continue making more advanced robots, you will need to master the power of object oriented programming.

The third major section of this book dealt with the basics of electricity and taught you everything you need to know before you can start building cool projects. We discussed the basic concepts behind electricity and how to protect yourself and the Pi from accidents. Safety instruction is crucial when working with electricity, hot solder, and glues. You can easily hurt yourself, damage your health, or at the very least damage your project. So take adequate precautions and stay safe. In this section you also received some guidance about the tools you will need for many projects. Creating cool Raspberry Pi gadgets involves much more than just programming. You get to solder connectors, sensors, and servo motors, and for that you need high quality tools.

Last but not least, we went through several projects that are meant to put your knowledge to the test. We started out with an easy to create, but handy web crawling bot and ended with a radio control plane than can survey and record the land. These projects prove the power behind Python as a programming language and the versatility of the Raspberry Pi.

All of this might seem a bit overwhelming, because there's a lot of information to digest. However, you should look at it as a personal challenge, and you will be able to build anything with the Pi. This little computer will help you build pretty much anything you can dream of. So put your programmer hat on, grab a soldering iron, and build cool robots that will take over the world for you!

www.ingramcontent.com/pod-product-compliance
Lightning Source LLC
Chambersburg PA
CBHW071202050326
40689CB00011B/2212